ENDORSEMENTS

Janet Boynes wisely suggests that the church's best strategy for dealing with the gay agenda is to "raise the standard of righteousness without condemning or hating those engaging in those behaviors." Delivered from homosexuality many years ago, Janet offers spiritual guidance to people wanting to break free from sexual sins, parents who don't know how to respond to their children's decisions and believers who need more knowledge about LGBT issues. This is a good resource that lovingly points readers to truth.

JAMES ROBISON
Founder and President, LIFE Outreach International
Fort Worth, Texas

Janet Boynes is living proof of God's unrelenting and transformational love. In a day of confusion, I am so thankful that her story is equipping leaders and parents with wisdom and hope. If you are in a position of leadership over people struggling with their sexuality, this book is a must read.

JOHN BEVERE
Author/Minister
Messenger International

Janet Boynes is light in the midst of darkness. Her personal narrative reconciles truth with love while her testimony serves as a clarion call for sexual purity in a world of moral relativism and decadence. This book will equip you to build a biblical firewall against an unprecedented assault on God's standards for sex, family, and culture.

REV. DR. SAMUEL RODRIGUEZ
President
NHCLC/CONELA
Hispanic Evangelical Association
Latinoevangelicals.com

The very thought of facing homosexuality, whether in the home or in the pulpit, makes many Christians panic. However, this is an ever-increasing factor in our society; none of us can run or hide any longer. Knowing what the Word of God says takes away *all* the fear. Janet Boynes' book, *God & Sexuality* sweetly, kindly, lovingly, but authoritatively walks anyone from zero knowledge to equipped to reach out with the love of God. Here is a book which points the way to compassion without compromise—just like Jesus! An easy reading handbook, it is a must for everyone seeking to know the freedom that truth brings.

PASTOR TERRI COPELAND PEARSONS
Eagle Mountain International Church

Janet's story of redemption is both captivating and inspiring. This book is filled with courage and compassion and will give you a better understanding on how to assist and walk alongside a loved one or friend who is struggling with same-sex attraction. It will also equip pastors and ministry leaders by teaching them how to speak the truth in love. We are living in times where we cannot afford to be oblivious toward what is going on around us, because the world needs to hear that Jesus still saves and sets the captives free.

DAVID BENHAM
www.BenhamBrothers.com
@DavidDBenham

I have come to know and trust Janet Boynes' courageous heart and message, which is laid out in this book. She is a strong lighthouse that stands on God's Word in the midst of a massive hurricane of today's hot topics of sexuality and gender. The light she sends out is hope and help for individuals and families that struggle in these areas. She's been there and has a voice that needs to be heard. You will be educated and encouraged by this book and her ministry.

PASTOR REBECCA WILSON LCSW, LMFT

This book is a godsend for Christian families whose children have chosen a LGBT lifestyle. It's a vitally important and informative resource, written with compassion and understanding by people who have traveled this journey and have answers. I couldn't recommend this book more.

KAREN JENSEN SALISBURY
Minister/Author

I want to commend Janet for being a forerunner for truth. Janet's personal testimony solidifies that an intimate relationship with Christ leads to transformation, deliverance, and freedom. Her courage to share her message in a time when the redemptive grace of God is overshadowed by rhetoric and a need to be politically correct should be applauded. Janet's message of compassion without compromise offers insight to the body of Christ to empower us to reach those that need to break free from a homosexual lifestyle.

LADY GAIL JOHNSON
First Lady of Pleasant Hill Church of Deliverance

GOD & THE
LGBT
COMMUNITY

GOD & THE
LGBT
COMMUNITY

A COMPASSIONATE GUIDE FOR
PARENTS, FAMILIES, & CHURCHES

JANET BOYNES

Published by Harrison House Publishers
Shippensburg, PA 17257

Cover design by Eileen Rockwell

13 digit ISBN: 9781680317749
Ebook 13 ISBN: 9781680317756
POD LP ISBN: 9781680317763
POD HC ISBN: 9781680317770

For Worldwide Distribution, Printed in the U.S.A.
1 2 3 4 5 6 7 8 / 25 24 23 22 21

Acknowledgments

This book was written for parents and ministry leaders who have contacted this ministry asking for help in how they should respond to their children who have chosen the homosexual lifestyle. My concern for these families inspired me to write a book so that they would have a tangible resource to help them in their journey.

To Eleanor Boynes, my mother, who went home to be with the Lord, you encouraged me to share our story. Thank you for the inspiration you have been to me. I love you, Mom.

This book would not have come to fruition without a team of generous people who offered their time and insight. Thank you: Alciona Rivera, Tim and Janet Distel, and Barb Anderson, your work demonstrates your concern for those who struggle with homosexuality. I appreciate and love you all.

Thank you to all our JBM volunteers who, day in and day out, pour out themselves to see lives changed and restored. Elicia Brown, Charlie Hernandez, and my amazing board you are the best!

Dr. Michael Brown, words cannot express my gratitude to you for your professional advice and assistance with this book.

To all who allowed me to share your personal stories in this book, thank you. You will not know the full impact that your story will have on those who read this book until you stand before the Lord.

CONTENTS

FOREWORD

This is an important book written by a remarkable woman, and if you're looking for a volume that deals with the toughest questions surrounding homosexuality—the questions that parents and siblings and pastors and counselors ask, the practical, personal questions—then this is the book for you. It is filled with scriptural wisdom and Christlike compassion, and that is because it is written by a woman who understands.

Janet's siblings had the same mother but different fathers, and one of those fathers sexually abused Janet when she was a child. Some years later, Janet left the man she was engaged to marry and began to live as a lesbian, disobeying the Lord she once knew and giving herself to drugs and to other women for 14 years. That's why I say that Janet understands.

She understands the struggles experienced by those in the LGBT community, being able to relate to the rejection they often experience at the hands of the Church and being able to identify with their wounds and their pain. (Janet invited Walt Heyer, a former male to female transgender, to speak first-hand to the "T" issues in the pages that follow.) But she also understands the ways of the Lord. She understands the power of prayer. She understands what it takes to hold fast to God's promises no matter what we feel or see. She understands how families can be torn apart, and she understands how they can be put back together.

In fact, as I read this book, I found myself asking, "Where did Janet get such practical wisdom and insight? Growing up the way she did and living for so many years in the world, how is she able to offer such excellent counsel?"

The answer is that Janet really knows the Lord, and through her walk with Him, she has learned His ways. It's also obvious that she has surrounded herself with godly leaders who have been able to speak into her life, helping her grow into a real woman of God. And it's obvious that her love for the LGBT community has moved her to make a real difference in their lives, raising up a ministry devoted to helping them find new life in Jesus and offering counsel to many hurting people in recent years.

So, she writes from personal experience, having "been there and done that" in many respects, from the lesbian lifestyle to her new life in the Lord to her ministry to those in need. And out of that personal experience, she has written a book that will be a lifesaver for many. There is a reason you're reading this book, and I believe you will find the answers you need in the chapters that follow.

DR. MICHAEL L. BROWN
Author, radio host, theologian, and activist
AskDrBrown.org

FOREWORD

I believe homosexuality has become the tip of the spear in Satan's assault today. If we don't blunt this point of attack, our society won't last. This is just the beginning. Yet how and what do we do? There is no unified Christian response to this issue, and sadly, there hasn't been much material available on this topic as Christian leaders chose to largely ignore the subject. Janet Boynes' book, *God & Sexuality*, is an attempt to fill that void.

Janet deals with the subject scripturally and leaves no room for doubt on what the Bible says. Yet she presents these truths in love, having been on both sides of the fence. She includes testimonies from families that have been dealing with family members caught up in this lifestyle for decades and there are also testimonies from those who have been liberated from the LGBT deception.

She lovingly calls Christians to take a stand while not condemning those caught in this trap. There is a lot of practical wisdom on how Christians should respond to those who are being destroyed by this "new morality."

Many have just accepted the situation as the new "norm" but it doesn't have to be. The Gospel is the most powerful force in the world. We have the truth. We just need to use it. Janet's book will encourage you and help equip you to make a difference. Individual lives and our society depends on it.

ANDREW WOMMACK
Andrew Wommack Ministries, Author

PREFACE

It is hard to believe you are about to read my third book. There are no words to describe what it feels like to be in this season in my life: writing books, speaking to churches and ministering to hundreds of people who have struggled or are struggling with homosexuality and want to leave the lifestyle once and for all. My story is about the painful consequences when we choose a life outside the will of God, yet there is freedom and peace in Christ.

Some people have asked why I think I am qualified to write this book. That is a good question. This book has been on my heart for a long time. There has never been a greater time in our history to present a book for parents, pastors, and the body that teaches on the issue of homosexuality. It isn't just because I lived the lifestyle for 14 years, although I know what I am talking about when I share the destruction a homosexual lifestyle can bring. Nor is it about experience speaking or leading a ministry that helps churches understand that our best and greatest hope to win the homosexual community to Christ is for us to consistently live a life of love and righteousness. But it is about being called of God; I have not only been called out of a homosexual lifestyle, but I have been called to an anointed life of helping others be set free.

Back in July of 2011, I received a powerful prophecy, the kind that shakes you up from the inside out and provides another piece of the puzzle for your life. The pastor shared about coming out of the darkness, new opportunities, and healing ministry. And then he said this, "Recognize the authority in which I've given you to walk." Authority. There it is. Why am I qualified to write this book? Because God has given me the authority. This is not an easy ministry to do. There are friends, family, and a large portion of the Church today who do not support me. Yet daily God gives me the strength to continue. And I will continue in the authority He has given me to speak His words of liberty.

INTRODUCTION

The issue of homosexuality is alive and well in our society today. It actually feels like a living, breathing dragon, consuming anything in its path that disagrees with the gay, lesbian, and transgender agenda. It attacks religious freedom and anyone who professes the belief that marriage is between one man and one woman.

How did we get this far? Why the need for this book? As a minister of the Gospel, I have been asked many times for something tangible to hand out that will help a parent, teacher, pastor, or family member not only understand what the issue is, but how to help the person involved. It is not a simple "pat on the shoulder and everything is going to be okay" solution. It has escalated to the point of an all-out war between political parties, fathers and sons, mothers and daughters, families, the Church, society, and God.

Matthew 10:21-22 says, "A brother will betray his brother to death, a father will betray his own child, and children will rebel against their parents and cause them to be killed. And all nations will hate you because you are my follower. But everyone who endures to the end will be saved" (NLT).

The message of this book is not about guilt or condemnation for a lifestyle choice. It is to share God's original intent for all humankind with regard not only to redemption but to living a life full of promise and freedom.

I also do not want to dictate how you handle family affairs. My desire is to give you biblical insight that can be helpful in making decisions you never thought you'd have to make. I want to provide you with the information, but you need to seek the Holy Spirit as to how to use it.

I encourage you to join me in prayer as you read this book and begin to deal with this difficult issue.

> *Dear Holy Spirit, I ask You to open my eyes as I read this book. Reveal Your truth, and grant me wisdom to honor You with my words and actions. I pray that I would be a reflection of Your love to those around me. Help me to forgive and seek forgiveness. Teach my heart to trust You and teach me to fix my eyes on You. In Jesus' name, Amen.*

| Part 1 |

THE PERSON

Chapter 1

Did God Make Me This Way?

This question is a great place to start, as it is on the minds of many who are struggling. The thought process is: "If God actually made me this way, it can't be wrong." However, someone who believes this probably has not taken into account the societal and environmental factors that have contributed to their belief system. It can be confusing for someone who is hearing opinions such as, "gay people are born that way," or "a person can transition back and forth between heterosexuality and homosexuality." Oftentimes, a person may just be listening to the opinions of others who tell them they must be gay because of their interests or mannerisms. In addition, there are often common threads in the life of a homosexual such as an absent parent, sexual or physical abuse, or some other dysfunction in the home. The Bible assures us that God knows who we are created to be. In Jeremiah 1:5, we are told, "Before I shaped you in the womb, I knew all about you" (MSG).

I believe it is best to turn to the Bible to properly answer this question. Let's start first with the story of creation, which was God's blueprint for the world before the entrance of sin.

Genesis 1:27-28 says, "So God created mankind in his own image; in the image of God he created them; male and female he created them. God blessed them and said to them, 'Be fruitful and increase in number; fill the earth and subdue it. Rule over the fish in the sea and the birds in the sky and over every living creature that moves on the ground'" (NIV).

Heterosexual relationships were designed as a model for all humanity, according to the creation account, and no mention was made of a homosexual union. Male and female is the only possible pairing that could allow mankind to be fruitful and multiply over the earth. The heterosexual model for relationships is repeated throughout Scripture as God's plan for marriage and family.

Jesus, in speaking of marriage and divorce to the Pharisees, said this in Matthew 19:4-6, "'Haven't you read,' he replied, 'that at the beginning the Creator "made them male and female" and said, "For this reason a man will leave his father and mother and be united to his wife, and the two will become one flesh"? So they are no longer two, but one flesh. Therefore what God has joined together, let no one separate'" (NIV).

This is such a powerful statement. We need to step back and carefully consider these words. Some argue that Jesus didn't mention homosexuality; but in these verses of Scripture, He takes us back to the creation of man and woman and says that from the beginning, we were created male and female, and because of this, a man will leave his parents and begin a brand-new partnership with a woman and the two shall become one flesh. Jesus declared that the intent of creation was for man and woman to be united. This *is* the purpose of God. Paul also reaffirms this in Ephesians 5:31, using the exact same wording. Both Jesus and Paul are promoting a heterosexual union through marriage. No mention is made of homosexual relationships, and their absence speaks loudly that they were not a part of God's plan.

If God did not create homosexuality, where did it come from? The fall of mankind in the Garden of Eden started a cycle of sin that fed upon itself. As sin grew, the more entrapped we became. Paul describes the process in Romans 1:20-32 (MSG):

> *But God's angry displeasure erupts as acts of human mistrust and wrongdoing and lying accumulate, as people try to put a shroud over truth. But the basic reality of God is plain enough. Open your eyes and there it is! By taking a long and thoughtful look at what God has created, people have always been able to see what their eyes as such can't see: eternal power, for instance, and the mystery of his divine being. So nobody has a good excuse. What happened was this: People knew God perfectly well, but when they didn't treat him like God, refusing to worship him, they trivialized themselves into silliness and confusion so that there was neither sense nor direction left in their lives. They pretended to know it all, but were illiterate regarding life. They traded the glory of God who holds the whole world in his hands for cheap figurines you can buy at any roadside stand. So God said, in effect, "If that's what you want, that's what you get." It wasn't long before they were*

living in a pigpen, smeared with filth, filthy inside and out. And all this because they traded the true God for a fake god, and worshiped the god they made instead of the God who made them—the God we bless, the God who blesses us. Oh, yes!

Worse followed. Refusing to know God, they soon didn't know how to be human either—women didn't know how to be women, men didn't know how to be men. Sexually confused, they abused and defiled one another, women with women, men with men—all lust, no love. And then they paid for it, oh, how they paid for it—emptied of God and love, godless and loveless wretches.

Since they didn't bother to acknowledge God, God quit bothering them and let them run loose. And then all hell broke loose: rampant evil, grabbing and grasping, vicious backstabbing. They made life hell on earth with their envy, wanton killing, bickering, and cheating. Look at them: mean-spirited, venomous, fork-tongued God-bashers. Bullies, swaggerers, insufferable windbags! They keep inventing new ways of wrecking lives. They ditch their parents when they get in the way. Stupid, slimy, cruel, cold-blooded. And it's not as if they don't know better. They know perfectly well they're spitting in God's face. And they don't care—worse, they hand out prizes to those who do the worst things best!

(Also see 2 Peter 1:3 and 2 Timothy 1:7.)

According to this passage of Scripture, homosexuality came about because of the persistence of mankind in sin. Individuals sought to replace the natural union God had created between man and woman with unnatural ones. God allowed it because they had already rejected Him in their hearts. He would not force them to love Him, and so He gave them over to their sins, even though the consequence of sin is death.

The consequence of sin is death, yet God did not abandon mankind to sin. His love for us wouldn't allow it. He sent His perfect Son to earth to suffer the death that should have been ours, taking our place. Because of Jesus' sacrifice, Romans 10:9 says, "If you declare with your mouth, 'Jesus is Lord,' and believe in your heart that God raised him from the dead, you will be saved" (NIV).

All people (whether homosexuals, murderers, adulterers, thieves, liars, or any other kind of sinner) can approach the throne of God and be forgiven for their sins by believing in the name of Jesus. God did not create people to be gay; He created them to be free from sin.

For many, struggling with homosexuality has been a lifelong conflict. We aren't here to say that their struggle isn't real. It is. We are here to offer them (you) the gift of Jesus. Jesus our Healer, Jesus the Mender of the broken, Jesus our Redeemer, Friend, and Savior. A revelation of His love for us is what compels us to pursue Him, and in doing so, we become whole. Many people think the goal of my ministry is to help people change from gay to straight, but they are missing the point. The ultimate goal is not to see people come out of homosexuality, but into wholeness in Christ.

Chapter 2

I WANT YOU TO SUPPORT ME

We are physical and emotional beings, created in the image of God. We have basic physical needs for such things as food, water, and air. We also have emotional needs for such things as validation, security, and approval. One of the most essential of these needs is our desire to be validated and supported in who we are and the decisions we make. We seek that validation and support from those closest to us. For example, a teenager wants approval from his peers, a wife seeks it from her husband, and children want parental approval. Our children want us to support them, including supporting their sexual identity. Their peers approve. Society approves. Even now, more and more churches are approving and performing same-sex marriages. So why can't their parents and/or family come alongside them and accept their choice of sexuality?

If there is a good relationship already established between the parent and the child, open communication, mutual respect, and "agreeing to disagree" often become the foundation or ground rules of the relationship. It is important for parents to be parents, especially when an underage child is involved. Our children may not like how we handle situations, but a parent cannot allow disrespect to be a standard in the relationship.

> *Honor your father and your mother, so that you may live long in the land the LORD your God is giving you.*
> EXODUS 20:12 NIV

How many times did you seek the approval or support of your parents? Jesus was even validated by His Father: "This is my dearly loved Son, who brings me great joy" (Matthew 3:17, NLT). Loving gay children does not mean you condone their choices. Acceptance is not the same as approval. Although they may demand your support of their lifestyle choice, do not cave in or allow them to manipulate you. Be consistent in your decision to love them without compromising the gospel of Jesus.

One mistake that parents and society make is to quickly label a young person as a homosexual because they do not fit the normal gender stereotypes that most children choose. For example, a young boy might prefer to dance, sing, and enjoy the arts over baseball or football. Many young girls want to play sports and are interested in working with tools instead of playing piano or dancing. Some young adults who struggle with same-sex attraction might have detached or separated from their true masculine or feminine identities. In other words, their outward appearance and speech may not match what is typically associated with a man or woman. Wise parents should encourage the gifts and talents their children possess while being careful not to belittle them because their interests differ from their peers or siblings.

Many young people may begin to explore homosexuality because of sexual abuse, rejection, abandonment, same-sex parents, exposure to pornography, or something as simple as name calling. A sensitive parent should be aware of this possibility and be ready to give support during this time.

The Amplified version of Proverbs 22:6 says that a parent should "Train up a child in the way he should go [and in keeping with his individual gift or bent]." When it comes to supporting our children's unique gifts, we should definitely reinforce them. It is an entirely different matter, however, when our child desires our support for the gay lifestyle.

See your child as a person, not just as a homosexual. I realize this is a tough chapter. It will be hard for many families and loved ones to love but not condone. We will get into this more in later chapters. The main purpose of this chapter is to encourage parents and families that it is possible to love our kids despite some of their choices.

So we love our children, or anyone for that matter, who is choosing to live a homosexual lifestyle or is struggling with same-sex attraction. We look for ways to validate them in their talents, gifts, opportunities, or health choices. At some point, and even before we can begin to pray for them, we need to examine our own hearts and forgive our children or relatives for anything we feel they may have done to us. You may feel like they have failed you and/or disappointed you. You may feel like they have trampled over your heart and shattered the dreams you had for them. Forgiveness truly sets us free to move and flow in our prayers with God and establishes the foundation to be kind and compassionate according to the Bible.

Chapter 3

CAN I STILL BE A CHRISTIAN AND BE GAY?

(UNDERSTANDING BIBLICAL ARGUMENTS)

You can't live a homosexual lifestyle and have an abundant, victorious Christian life!

There are many voices today in our culture. The media, movies, political and educational systems, and even some churches try to influence our beliefs and attitudes regarding homosexuality with views that are not based on a sound biblical understanding. Even well-intentioned people such as family and friends can give advice lacking biblical truth. Without a foundation based on Scripture, we become "tossed back and forth by the waves, and blown here and there by every wind of teaching and by the cunning and craftiness of people in their deceitful scheming" (Ephesians 4:14, NIV). Therefore, this is a very difficult question to answer.

All sin separates us from God, for He cannot tolerate sin in His presence. Both the Old and New Testaments define homosexuality as a sin. The Bible is not unclear about this. Some argue that there is very little said about it in Scripture, but this is not true. Here are a few passages: Genesis 19:1-11; Leviticus 18:22; Judges 19:16-24; Romans 1:18-32; 1 Corinthians 6:9-11; 1 Timothy 1:8-10; and Jude 7.

There are people, even some pastors, who waver or distort Scripture regarding the subject of homosexuality even though the Bible is very clear. People who twist and manipulate the Word to fit their own desires or preconceived ideas are not a new phenomenon. We see that correction had to be brought to the Galatians because they began to leave the truth of the gospel for a different "gospel." There were some people who began to confuse the believers by altering the gospel of Christ. Paul's message to them was that if he, or even an angel from heaven began to preach a different gospel contrary to the one they received, consider the messenger to be "accursed" (Galatians 1:7-8).

Some people alter their beliefs because they want to please and be accepted by others. They don't want to appear as if they are outside the fashionable crowd. But our goal must be to seek the favor of God not man. Paul said that if he strived to please men, he wouldn't be a true servant of Christ. Popular culture never changes truth; instead, truth needs to change popular culture.

Yes, it is tough to stand up against culture. We all want to be liked and accepted, but it's a stand we must take. The world will always try to press you into its mold. People even resort to bullying, ridicule, and name-calling if you stand up for biblical truth. However, Jesus' words ring true when He said, "If they persecuted me, they will persecute you also" (John 15:20, NIV). Christians are called to be overcomers even in the midst of pressure situations.

Whenever you hear someone try to justify a sin by manipulating or explaining away a verse of Scripture, a red flag should instantly go up. If you try to convince yourself that God really said something, then it's time to stop and get your heart right before God.

In Genesis 3:1, the devil asked Eve, "Did God really say," and it got her in a lot of trouble. Let's use her life as an example. Justifying a sin is dangerous because our hearts and minds can become hardened toward the things of God. Always keep your heart open and pliable before Him.

Paul, without a doubt, classifies homosexuality as a sin. In Romans 1:25, he states that some people exchanged the truth of God for a lie. They abandoned the natural function of intercourse between male and female and, instead, committed acts men with men and woman with woman. He distinguishes between what is "natural" and what is a "lie." Someone who practices this way of life without turning from it will come under judgment.

A very telling account of God's judgment is seen in Genesis chapters 18 and 19. "The outcry against Sodom and Gomorrah is so great and their sin so grievous that I will go down and see if what they have done is as bad as the outcry that has reached me. If not, I will know" (Genesis 18:20-21, NIV). The Lord sent two angels who had the appearance of men to these two cities to confirm if the sin was, indeed, as bad as it appeared. The two angels planned to spend the night at the home of Abraham's nephew, Lot. Yet many men of the city surrounded Lot's home and demanded that Lot send the two men out to them so that they could have intercourse with them. The angels struck the men of the city with blindness. They told Lot and his family to immediately get out of the city because the outcry of sin was confirmed and judgment was about to fall. Fire and brimstone rained down on the cities, and they were destroyed.

I would like to point out two important facts revealed in this account. First, according to the biblical passages, homosexuality was the primary sin that the angels encountered in the cities, and that experience sealed God's judgment on the people. Second, the Genesis account states that the angels sought out anyone who was righteous in the cities. God is not willing for any person to perish but extends forgiveness to anyone who repents and turns from sin.

God gave Moses many laws regarding immoral relations. In Leviticus 18:22, God told Moses that a male shall not lie with another male as he does with a female. This is a straightforward law from God and isn't subject to any misinterpretation. Sexual relations between two people of the same sex was, and still is, forbidden.

In addition to specific biblical passages forbidding homosexuality, there is the totality of Scripture that supports those verses. In Genesis 2:24, God said that a man shall leave his father and mother and be joined to his wife. He did not say he is to be joined to another man. This husband and wife, man and woman structure in marriage is seen throughout the entire Bible.

Peter discussed healthy family relationships in 1 Peter 3:1-9. The whole foundation of the family structure is set in the context of a man and a woman. Jesus himself put His stamp of approval on the institution of marriage consisting of a man and a woman in Matthew 19:3-6. Jesus also confirmed the will of God by quoting Genesis 2:24; a man leaves his parents and joins himself to a woman. That's a huge insurmountable fact to dismiss.

Detailed advice is given for marriage in 1 Corinthians 7. Sexual relationships and guidelines are discussed. These are entirely applied to a man and a woman. Death of a spouse, remarriage, divorce, and separation are all in the context of a man and a woman. If homosexual relationships were accepted, then all of the teachings on marriage and the principles illustrated throughout the Bible would not be solely framed, as they definitely are, to a male and a female.

If we accept Scripture as truth, then a person needs to forsake sin. The good news is that Jesus' death on the cross paid the penalty of all sin, including homosexuality. Paul states in 1 Corinthians 6:10-11 that we should not allow ourselves to be deceived. Homosexuals, among others, shall not inherit the Kingdom of God. *But*, those who have lived that lifestyle can be washed and rendered innocent by Jesus' sacrifice. In fact, some of the Corinthians Paul was writing to were formerly living the homosexual life. They were called out, and they responded.

It's important to bear in mind that a Christian can still be tempted with homosexuality. Being tempted, in and of itself, is not sinful. Jesus was tempted in *every* way that we are, yet

He didn't give in. Sound friendships and solid church involvement, as well as continually being immersed in prayer and Bible study, will lessen and overcome the power of temptation.

What if a Christian gives in and commits a homosexual act? That person does not become a Christian homosexual. He must confess and repent of that sin, and God will cleanse him from all unrighteousness (1 John 1:9). It is only when a person "practices" sin that they are in serious danger, and it reveals their heart is not right with God (1 John 3:8-10).

Here lies the critical distinction between a Christian who loves God yet falls into a sin, versus someone who calls himself a Christian but habitually sins and does not seriously ask for forgiveness. The former person needs to repent and grow in respect with God. That person may need to seek out help from other mature believers. Whereas, the latter person is deceiving himself, and we must pray for his eyes to be opened.

There are several decisions or habits that people must integrate into their life in order to gain victory over temptation. First and foremost, they must immerse their hearts and minds in God's Word. When Jesus was tempted by the devil in Matthew 4, He responded to each temptation by quoting Scripture. The Word of God is called, "the sword of the Spirit." It's an offensive weapon that will destroy every ungodly thought that is thrown at you. David said, "I have hidden your word in my heart that I might not sin against you" (Psalm 119:11, NIV).

Second, it's vital to connect to a Bible-believing church. God has placed pastors and leaders in the church who will minister to your life. Putting yourself in a place where you'll receive encouragement will help ensure success in your Christian walk. Getting involved in a small group where you are accountable to others is very helpful. But you must also be willing to serve others in some area of ministry. Blessings will be reaped when you focus on the needs of other people.

Surrounding yourself with positive people is only part of the solution. Negative influences also need to be cut off from your life. Old friendships and hang-outs that were a part of your past will need to be left behind. The Bible says not to team up with darkness (2 Corinthian 6:14). Pray for your former acquaintances (friends), but you must not subject yourself to an atmosphere that will draw you away from walking a holy life. The Internet and certain websites are often sources of temptation. You must submit those areas to God.

Set aside time to pray every day. Lack of one-on-one time with God in prayer will result in spiritual weakness. This makes you more susceptible (vulnerable) to temptation. Jesus told His disciples in Luke 22:40 to pray so they would not fall or give in to temptation. A life without prayer is like a car without gas—you won't get to your destination.

Others argue that God is love and His grace will cover them no matter how they live their lives. God certainly is love. He loves us so much that He has provided a way out of sin. His blood was shed to pave the way that will take us across the breach that sin creates. But we must follow His direction. We must receive His love. The choice is ours.

Paul, again, sheds light on this issue. He asks, "Can I sin because I live under the grace of God?" In the verses that follow, he answers by saying, "May it never be," or literally,

"God forbid" (Romans 6:1-7). We have to realize that it's the very love of God that is reaching out to us and imploring us to steer far from sin. God knows where sin desires to take us and where its end will be. Sin will take us further than we want to go and keep us longer than we want to stay.

When God instructs us not to partake in certain behaviors, people often misinterpret that by thinking that God just doesn't want us to have any fun. But think of it this way. When parents tell their young children not to leave the yard when they are playing outside, it's for the protection of the children, not to stifle the fun factor. They could be struck by a car or be a victim of abduction. God's commands are for our protection. Fulfillment comes to our lives when we do things according to His will.

The devil lies to us just as he did in the beginning when he asked Eve, "Did God really say you must not eat the fruit from the tree? You surely won't die." Adam and Eve believed the lie and the consequences were sin, struggle, heartache, disease, and banishment from the Garden of Eden. God's plan is for us to listen to His will and ask forgiveness for our sins, and He will deliver us from destruction.

The Christian life is all about becoming more like Christ. We are continually being transformed into His image as we follow His Word and forsake sin in our lives. John said, "I write this to you so that you will not sin" (1 John 2:1, NIV). In other words, we should not be living our lives in such a way that we're always pushing the limits or seeing how close we can come to sin.

In summary, people who have lived a homosexual lifestyle can, without a doubt, become a Christian or return to their Christian roots. Even though they become "new creations in Christ," that doesn't mean they will no longer be tempted and struggle. As they grow in their relationship with Christ and learn what the Bible teaches about homosexuality, they will need to lay aside the sin that has so easily entangled them (Hebrews 12:1).

On the other hand, those individuals who know what the Bible says regarding homosexuality and refuse to allow God to have that area of their life are in a dangerous position with God. It would be like someone who lives a lifestyle of adultery being called a Christian adulterer. The good news is that there will be many former homosexuals in heaven who have repented and given their lives to Christ.

Chapter 4

BECOMING AN OVERCOMER

(TO THE STRUGGLER)

To the struggler who grew up in a Christian home, to the one who up till now had no idea about the love of God, and to the one who still has questions if He is real—Jesus loves *you*. Your struggle is not a sign of anger from God. Your struggle is not a curse or punishment because of something you did or did not do. You are deeply loved with an unquenchable love that is so good, it's hard to believe. Matthew 11:28-30 in *The Message* says, "Are you tired? Worn out? Burned out on religion? Come to me. Get away with me and you'll recover your life. I'll show you how to take a real rest. Walk with me and work with me—watch how I do it. Learn the unforced rhythms of grace. I won't lay anything heavy or ill-fitting on you. Keep company with me and you'll learn to live freely and lightly."

Jesus is offering you rest for your soul, peace that can't be explained, and a joy that is unspeakable! This is what Jesus is offering you!

I won't disregard the weight of your pain by lecturing you or telling you to get over it. We both know that if it were that easy, you would not be reading this book. I do, however, want to share the beauty of the cross with you. What it means to bring our mess, our baggage, and our shame to the feet of the cross of Jesus where freedom is granted and not earned.

Seeing Jesus for who He truly is removes every ounce of hesitation. Surrender becomes a delight in light of His precious gift of life. Following Christ can sometimes be painted as a dreadful experience, when in fact, it is exhilarating and adventurous.

God's take on homosexuality is clear, and I don't need to remind you of that. We know where He stands on the issue. Let me remind you, however, that He doesn't condemn you to a life of misery and never-ending struggle. His invitation goes further than just offering you forgiveness. His invitation is for you to live a life of prosperity and victory here on earth.

While being financially stable is great, that's not all I mean when I say prosperity. Prospering is being successful, flourishing, and thriving in every area of your life. As children of God, we are not designed to live apart from Him, although many of us do not live the life for which we are destined.

You may ask, how does this help me with my same-sex attraction? Knowing God is the key. Your perspective of who He is will either draw you to Him or move you away from Him. Focusing on Jesus and all that He says about you, fixing your eyes on Him and all that He offers you, rather than constantly trying to change how you feel, makes all the difference.

If you struggle with pornography and you really try to stop watching it, for a week or a month, you might be able to do it. However, I can guarantee you that you will go back to watching porn. Why? Because the need that drove you to it is still there.

I don't want you to focus on your weaknesses and struggles. The key is to pursue Jesus wholeheartedly. He asks that we love Him with all our heart, soul, strength, and mind. If we are conscious about this, and we are living purposely for Him, I can promise you that everything else will fade into the background. The chains that once bound you will no longer hold you. Only with Jesus' help can we overcome sin. Paul makes this point in Romans 7:17-25 (MSG):

> But I need something more! For if I know the law but still can't keep it, and if the power of sin with- in me keeps sabotaging my best intentions, I obviously need help! I realize that I don't have what it takes. I can will it, but I can't do it. I decide to do good, but I don't really do it. I decide not to do bad, but then I do it anyway. My decisions, such as they are, don't result in actions. Something has gone wrong deep within me and gets the better of me every time. It happens so regularly that it's predictable. The moment I decide to do good, sin is there to trip me up. I truly delight in God's commands, but it's pretty obvious that not all of me joins in that delight. Parts of me overtly rebels,

*and just when I least expect it, they take charge. I've
tried everything and nothing helps. I'm at the end
of my rope. Is there no one who can do anything for
me? Isn't that the real question? The answer, thank
God, is that Jesus Christ can and does. He acted to
set things right in this life of contradictions where I
want to serve God with all my heart and mind, but
I am pulled by the influence of sin to do something
totally different.*

The key to walking in complete victory over our sin, our
emotions, and fleshly struggles is agreeing with Jesus and
reinforcing sin's defeat in our own lives. "How do we do that?"
You are probably asking. The answer is that we focus, meditate, and speak out the promises found in God's Word that tell
us who we are in Christ.

There are dozens of verses in the Bible that include
the phrases, "In Him," and "In Christ." When temptation
comes our way, we should be prepared with specific verses of
Scripture that we are ready to meditate on and say aloud.

Remember, Jesus was tempted by the devil in the wilderness in Matthew chapter 4. For each temptation that came
against Him, He quoted a verse of scripture back at the
tempter. Ephesians 6:10-18 lists for us all the spiritual weapons that are at our disposal. Verse 17 says that we must take
the sword of the Spirit, which is the Word of God. We must
use it.

Jesus already stripped the devil of his authority, and now
we, as Christians, need to enforce the devil's defeat by using

our weaponry. Remember that Jesus said in Mark 11:23, "Truly I tell you, if anyone says to this mountain, 'Go, throw yourself into the sea,' and does not doubt in their heart but believes that what they say will happen, it will be done for them" (NIV). God wants you to be an overcomer. He didn't say you should dwell on the size of the obstacle. He loves you and has compassion on you in the midst of your struggle to change.

Let's look at the process of change. There was a man in the Bible called Naaman. He was the commander of the armies of the king of Aram. He was a valiant soldier, but he had leprosy. There was a girl who had been taken from Israel and was forced to serve Naaman's wife. She told her mistress that if Naaman would go see the prophet, he would cure him of his leprosy. Naaman went and told the king of Aram about what he had heard, and the king encouraged him to go to the prophet and sent him with a letter.

> *When the king of Israel read the letter, he tore his clothes in dismay and said, "Am I God that I can give life and take it away? Why is this man asking me to heal someone with leprosy? I can see that he's just trying to pick a fight with me."*
>
> *But when Elisha, the man of God, heard that the king of Israel had torn his clothes in dismay, he sent this message to him; "Why are you upset? Send Naaman to me and he will learn that there is a true prophet here in Israel."*
>
> *So Naaman went with his horses and chariots and waited at the door of Elisha's house. But Elisha sent*

a messenger out to him with this message: "Go and wash yourself seven times in the Jordan River. Then your skin will be restored, and you will be healed of your leprosy."

But Naaman became angry and stalked away. "I thought he would certainly come out to meet me!" He said. "I expected him to wave his hand over the leprosy and call on the name of the LORD his God and heal me! Aren't the rivers of Damascus, the Abana and the Pharpar, better than any of the rivers of Israel? Why shouldn't I wash in them and be healed?" So Naaman turned and went away in a rage.

2 KINGS 5:7-12 NLT

How many times have you asked God to remove the same-sex attraction and set you free? We know that He is all powerful, so why can't He just say the words? I understand. I have been there. I believe that He is more interested in seeing us through our struggle than taking us out of it. There are characteristics of who He is that He wants to reveal to us in the midst of our pain. He did not cause the pain, but He will never leave us or abandon us in it. Often the process can get the best of us. Naaman was given a way out, a solution to his leprosy. How many times has God given us a solution that we didn't like? For whatever reason, it was not how we thought it should be, and we became angry at God and the process.

But the story doesn't end there.

But his officers tried to reason with him and said, "Sir, if the prophet had told you to do something very difficult, wouldn't you have done it? So you should certainly obey him when he says simply, 'Go and wash and be cured!'" So Naaman went down to the Jordan River and dipped himself seven times, as the man of God had instructed him. And his skin became as healthy as the skin of a young child, and he was healed!

2 Kings 5:13-14 NLT

Your process will look different than mine. What God is asking of you in your journey to wholeness will be different from what He is asking of me. Don't quit because the healing pain feels like too much to endure. Isn't someone who has undergone surgery to fix a physical problem still in pain for a while after the surgery has been completed? In the same way, once Jesus mends our broken hearts, there will be evidence of the work that He has done. It's a good pain. It's a pain that will not last. Don't give up on Jesus. Don't allow your pride to drive you to turn away in rage like Naaman initially did. Your healing takes place from the inside out, because as I often say, God is not interested in behavior modification, He is interested in soul transformation. Allow the Holy Spirit to work in you. You are already the apple of His eye. Will you trust Him to carry you through? I promise He won't disappoint.

Chapter 5

DIALOGUE WITH YOUR CHILD ABOUT HIS OR HER LIFESTYLE CHOICE

Open communication with your children is vital if you want to know what is going on in their lives. The younger they are, the better the chances that you, as a parent, will recognize struggles that might be taking place inside their hearts and minds. Many young children will experience same-sex attraction because they admire certain qualities in their peers. Usually, this is not sexual in nature. Little boys shy away from girls thinking they have "cooties," and young girls feel the same way about boys. This is natural. It is very concerning, though, when a young boy who is attracted in a non-sexual way to another boy is told that he could be a homosexual.

The gay propaganda is rapidly spreading in schools, even on the elementary level. A young boy may be told that homosexuality is good and acceptable, which will send him into a confused state. After all, he doesn't like girls at this age and is drawn to other boys, so he may think, "I must be gay." As the parent, you should be alert to this possibility and be ready to explain the difference between same-sex attraction and homosexuality.

Same-sex attraction is misplaced desires for the same sex, which need to be given up to God. Committing to a homosexual lifestyle is an act of rebellion.

There are other behaviors that parents must examine in order to discover the source of their child's feelings. It is natural for children as they mature to spend more time alone in their room and less time with their family. However, if they begin acting unusually quiet, withdrawn, or they sleep a lot, it is time to explore the reason behind these behaviors. A child who is being sexually abused can display these symptoms.

Many instances of homosexuality can be traced to sexual abuse. It is vital that we approach our child to discover the source of the changes we may be observing. Almost without exception, the child will not volunteer the information that "Uncle so-and-so is touching me inappropriately." They are feeling vulnerable and, in many cases, guilty for what is taking place. Always keep your child's sexual safety in mind. It is also very necessary in this day and time to discuss what is appropriate and what is not, before any experiences take place. This gives your child the confidence to say "no" and to talk with you about what may be happening.

Sometimes the onset of puberty is delayed with certain individuals. There could be a medical reason for this, or it may merely be they are just maturing later. Regardless, this can be a deeply sensitive experience for a young person to endure. Be aware of the possibility that your child may be ridiculed. When your whole world revolves around your peers, their opinions matter. Encourage your child daily. If you have a young man, make him feel masculine. If you have a daughter, express to her that she is beautiful and worthy of tremendous respect.

Certain physical traits may be a source of self-doubt. A boy who is short or a girl who is unusually tall or small-breasted may question his or her identity. Your role as a parent in these situations cannot be underestimated.

An issue that often occurs is a child's seeming failure to live up to an older sibling's personality or accomplishments. An older brother is the star athlete on the school football team and everyone expects the same dazzling performance from the younger child, who fails to walk in his brother's shoes. Or, the younger sister who is more of an introvert gets compared to the outgoing, popular older sister. Society and even some parents unintentionally deflate the ego of the one while heaping praise on the other. In most instances, those "outcasts" possess amazing abilities and talents. Yet they are undiscovered, because they have given up on themselves or they are expected to engage in the same interests or have the same personality traits as their accomplished sibling.

A key factor in helping your child who is struggling with homosexuality is discovering what he believes the Bible teaches about the topic. Unfortunately, many parents lose their sons and daughters because the children have witnessed hypocrisy in the home or endured legalistic Christianity. Children might not respect the authority of Scripture due to its misuse or because they have witnessed inconsistent Christian behavior. If you are guilty of either of these two things, then repentance is in order, and you probably need to ask forgiveness from your children.

How we express biblical truth is something each of us must evaluate. A parent who tries to teach that homosexuality is wrong by ridiculing homosexuals and name-calling will be ineffective in shaping their children's beliefs, or at the very least, it will give them a warped understanding about the heart of God. It is important that a parent take a child on a journey through Scripture, a journey that reveals homosexuality as a sin and how it is not a part of God's design for men and women, but at the same time, our children need to learn that Jesus loves the homosexual and shed His blood for each one of them, just as He did for us. This understanding should help the child be more receptive to discussions on the matter.

When exploring your older child's scriptural understanding of homosexuality, you are likely to discover he believes that it doesn't matter who gets married, just as long as they love each other. However, "love" is not a valid qualification for two people marrying. If it were, the same logic would allow three men to marry each other, a brother and sister to marry, and a man to marry two women. After all, how can you suddenly put restrictions on other peoples' preferences when you have changed the basis of marriage with "love" as the only standard? To be consistent, one must allow every form of "marriage" to be validated. Society would be thrown into chaos if this took place.

The importance of knowing what is going on in your child's thinking process cannot be overstated. There are those who, for a variety of reasons, seek to indoctrinate our impressionable children within the public school arena. The Christian viewpoint is increasingly at odds with what is taught in schools, projected by the media, and given public policy status by lawmakers. The gay-rights movement has a plan to transform society. A part of its plan is to indoctrinate impressionable kids from an early age to accept homosexuality as normal. As Christians, we must do everything we can to protect their minds and hearts from false teaching.

Parents often relinquish their children to the oversight and care of schools at increasingly younger ages. Schools are taking on the parental role, from feeding our children to forming their basic values and beliefs.

Anti-bullying lessons are used to crush dissent. Bullying should not be tolerated for any reason, even when gay activists use anti-bullying policies as a cloak to bully children and their parents into honoring and celebrating their lifestyle. If you stand for traditional values, you are labeled a homophobe, bigot, or hater. This, too, is bullying.

Being a parent in this type of atmosphere is a major challenge. We must be "wise as serpents" and "harmless as doves" (Matthew 10:16). Wisdom and discernment are required for parents to stay connected to their children.

| Part 2 |

THE FAMILY

| Chapter 6 |

KNOW YOUR ENEMY

(ATTACK ON THE FAMILY)

When a towering skyscraper is being constructed, the foundation is the most critical element. It's the load-bearing component upon which the entire structure rests. If the foundation is unstable, then the whole building is in danger of collapse. External pressures will soon take their toll on a building with a compromised substructure. Similarly, in order to have a healthy society, the basic foundation must be steadfast. The traditional family unit is that foundation.

Strong families result in stable societies and stable societies will positively influence nations. We learn from Scripture that Satan's nature is to kill, steal, and destroy (John 10:10). So it is not surprising that he would target the cornerstone of all that is good. He has taken aim at the very structure where an environment of happiness, personal maturity, and stability are best instilled. The traditional family is under relentless assault.

Some might say that our society is still free and prosperous and that it is basically stable. But I would argue that it takes a few years for the full effects of changing the institution of marriage to be seen. Consider the "cut flower" theory. A flower can be cut from its stem and still appear beautiful and healthy for a while, but given some time, it will begin to wilt and die. We, in the United States, have enjoyed bountiful blessings that few other societies have experienced. Our generation has reaped this prosperity, even though we have not always been a perfect nation. Our blessings are because our moral codes, family structure, and work ethic are all rooted in Judeo-Christian values. If we "cut off" our beliefs from the root of our biblical foundations, then our blessed society will begin to fade away and eventually deteriorate altogether.

Our country has increasingly experienced the consequences of a declining family structure. Many people of this generation take for granted our way of life in the United States. They do not make the connection between our freedoms and prosperity to the spiritual beliefs and sacrifice of those who preceded them. To ignore or change those things which built this country will result in a poorer, weaker nation, that can easily be overtaken by forces that intend to enslave and dominate us. This is already happening today.

Social revolutionaries have diabolically targeted marriage as a major strategy to accomplish their goals. I believe it is not a coincidence that we have seen a flood of sexual images in the media. Almost all movies integrate sexual plots. Recently, many sitcoms have displayed homosexual relationships as fulfilling and beautiful. A morally-depraved nation will become weak and easily controlled.

Paul, in 2 Timothy 3:1-5, lays out a list of behaviors that would signify the "last days." Some of these include men being lovers of self, children disobeying parents, ungratefulness, and hatred of good, and love of pleasure rather than love of God. The pervasiveness of sex before marriage, adultery, and homosexuality are truly fulfillments of Paul's inspired warning. Let me interject that the Church must extend grace and forgiveness to those who are living in these lifestyles. The Church must raise the standard of righteousness without condemning or hating those engaging in those behaviors. Jesus came for all sinners.

While we extend compassion for the sinner, we must also teach the sanctity of marriage. No other society in the history of humankind has accepted homosexual marriage as a substitute for traditional marriage. Incredibly, the consequences of such an action are barely discussed at all. This is astounding. The health of our society is based on the traditional family. Yet people eagerly dismiss any discussion of the negative impact that changing the definition of marriage will bring. Instead, many people resort to labeling those who stand for traditional marriage as haters and homophobes, instead of intellectually and spiritually seeking information about this crucial issue.

From the beginning of time, the traditional family unit, consisting of one man and one woman, has provided the best environment for a child to grow and mature into a thriving individual. A child in a same-sex household is denied either a father or a mother. To accept that this is not detrimental, you must believe that one of the genders brings nothing distinctive to the table as it relates to meeting the emotional, mental, and spiritual needs of a child. For instance, if two men are parenting a child, then the child never receives what a mother can uniquely contribute. To view this as acceptable, a person would have to believe that men and women are exactly the same and bring nothing unique to the child. The reality is, the child suffers. Single moms know how difficult it is not to have the influence of a father in their child's life. The same is true for single dads.

As I mentioned in my previous chapter, redefining marriage opens the door for other forms of marriage besides same-sex. For example, a man and two women, two men and two women, a man and a stepmother, or a brother and sister could marry. You may say, "That's ridiculous!" But is it? Wandering from the Judeo-Christian ethic leaves the door wide open. If the only qualification needed to allow marriage is that the participants "love" one another, as we are told is the case with same-sex marriage, then why not? Society would have cast off its mooring, and now the ship is free to go anywhere. During the time of the judges in the Old Testament, everyone did what was right in his own eyes because they had no king to lead them (Judges 17:6). People, left to their own devices apart from God, have no guardrails to keep them from eventually careening off the cliff.

Homosexual marriage is also harmful because it attempts to turn same-sex marriage into a civil rights issue instead of a moral one. The Bible does not forbid a person born white to marry a person born black. Skin color is a matter of birth and is amoral. Homosexuality, on the other hand, is a behavior and therefore, a choice. When homosexual marriage is labeled a civil rights issue, then those who disagree with the lifestyle are suddenly placed in the same category as a racist. That is the goal of the militant gay activists.

We have already witnessed a deputy clerk jailed, a major CEO forced to resign, a baker lose his business, and a reality television show cancelled—all because these people would not endorse same-sex marriage. Freedom of thought, belief, and religion are under assault. The same people who cry tolerance are some of the first people to shut down all dissenting opinions. This is a troublesome trend.

Marriage and family are experiencing another challenge in our educational systems. Two organizations—Gay, Lesbian and Straight Education Network (GLSEN) and Parents, Families, and Friends of Lesbians and Gays (PFLAG)—are both actively influencing the students in our schools. They use anti-bullying tactics to silence those who have a differing view of homosexuality. Under the guise of protecting gay students from bullying, no one is allowed to express their moral, Christian opposition to the lifestyle.

No one condones the bullying of anyone, but these organizations overreach and suppress speech. The goal of GLSEN is to change the paradigm of students' beliefs regarding homosexuality. As a result, a wedge is often driven between students and their parents. These groups promote early sex education with sexually explicit material and promote the "coming out" of students as well as encouraging homosexual practices at a young age. They encourage sexual experimentation and provide opportunities for youth who question their sexuality to meet with older individuals living the lifestyle.

Those who affirm homosexuality are viewed as the "cool parents," while those who hold Christian values are portrayed as the "hostile parents." They teach their own interpretation of Scripture on the subject of homosexuality, which collides with sound biblical truth.

This is just a sampling of the agenda goals they have in mind for our children. Jesus has prophesied that children would rise up against parents in the last days. Unfortunately, radical gay activists are negatively influencing our children at a time when the family structure is already unhealthy and unstable.

Will we, as Christians, allow our marriages and families to be ransacked? Will we stand strong in this day and declare truth in the face of an all-out assault? Our battle is spiritual in nature (2 Corinthians 10:3-5). Our marriages must be built on the Rock, Jesus Christ. Husbands and wives must renounce sin and guard themselves from the temptations of our culture, whose goal is to compromise our integrity. Believers are the salt and light in the world. Don't allow the saltiness to be diluted or the light to be shaded.

In the spirit of the love of God, we must speak truth to this generation. Compromise isn't the answer. It only encourages the other side to take more ground. Healthy marriages are the foundation of a healthy society. We must guard that institution from those who wish to transform it from God's original intent: one man and one woman.

Chapter 7

THE BLAME GAME

(ATTACK ON MARRIAGE)

Every responsible parent of a child struggling with homosexuality will eventually ask, "Did I contribute to my child's choice?" First of all, this is a healthy question to consider. An uncaring parent will not confront that possibility and instead will throw all the blame entirely onto the child or onto the spouse's actions or inactions. Of course, if any type of abuse was present in the home—sexual, physical, or emotional—then your child's behavior can most definitely be a response to that pain. Apart from abuse, parents who truly love their child will evaluate their own shortcomings that may have contributed a piece of the puzzle, even if it is a very small one. It's unhealthy, however, to go overboard and be under a cloud of condemnation. All parents make mistakes, and our children respond to them in different ways.

Stressful situations, like a child struggling with sexuality, will test both the strength of your marriage and your ability to present a unified course of action. But unity between spouses is vital. Division between a husband and wife can greatly affect the way a child will deal with same-sex attraction. The existence of perfect parents is a myth. Sometimes we look at other families and think that they have it made with no struggle and perfect children, but all families have their own set of problems. They just aren't visible to everyone else. You would be surprised to learn how many families share circumstances similar to the ones yours is experiencing.

One hurdle that must be overcome is the blame game between spouses. Success in dealing with your child's same-sex attraction will require godly maturity and most notably, a humble heart. Depending on the person, sometimes a parent looks inward and sees all of his/her own shortcomings that might have contributed to the child's struggle. Other times, a parent might ignore self-examination and instead project the failure completely on the spouse. A wise parent will receive correction from multiple sources: God, the inspired Word of God, their spouse, and other godly people. You can also learn from your child when they share their feelings. Paul told Timothy, "Pay close attention to yourself and your teaching" (1 Timothy 4:16, NLT). We should deal with the beam in our own eyes before we judge the splinter in our spouse's.

The goal here is the well-being of your child. So if the Holy Spirit is dealing with you concerning your anger, lack of warmth, belittling, favoritism of one child over another, controlling nature, lack of involvement, or emotional detachment, then be open to the correction. Remember, God disciplines those He loves. His conviction is for our own good.

How you approach your spouse is important. If you communicate in an accusatory way, then your spouse will have a closed heart and mind to the things that might need changing. However, if you first share what God is doing in you, it opens up the door to have a non-threatening conversation with your spouse.

While this book is not a manual for marriage, you will discover that the health of your marriage is central to your ability to come through the storm, which has broken upon you. It is interesting to witness the horrific recorded last moments before a plane crash—some passengers are praying to God while others are cursing in anger. When you experience the heart-wrenching situation of your child's disclosure, what impact will it have on your marriage? Will this drive a wedge between you and your spouse, or will you draw strength and comfort from each other?

Men: This is the time to be the godly leader that you are positioned to be. A godly leader doesn't need to force people to follow him, but instead he will draw his family to him by his Christlike behavior. Jesus is our perfect example of a true leader. First, He possessed great authority, yet His driving motivation was compassion and love. Second, He did not compromise the truth in the midst of opposition.

Husbands, according to 1 Peter 3:7, your prayers are hindered when you do not treat our wives the way that God intends. We know that prayer is the key to seeing the change you desire. So men, take a long hard look at how you are fulfilling your call as husbands and fathers. For some of you, there needs to be a drastic change in your attitude and behavior. Perhaps you have let your job or hobbies take precedence over God and your family.

I have a few questions for you. Are you treating your wife and children with gentleness and compassion? Are you spending time with your kids doing things they enjoy doing? Are you still "dating" your wife? You might say, "I would give my life for my family." But I ask you, will you live for them? Merely telling them about God is not enough. We need to live our Christianity in the home. As the saying goes, "Christianity is caught, not taught." So often, parents lose their children because of their lukewarm Christianity. Draw close to God in prayer and Scripture reading every day. Allow the Holy Spirit to bring change to your heart and life. The anointing of God on our lives will be required if we want to reach our children for God. You are in a spiritual battle, and your child's life is hanging in the balance.

Women: The position of a wife and mother is a very important position in the family. Women provide stability and cohesiveness in the home, and this role can make a huge difference in keeping the family together.

It is vital, first of all, to be in agreement with your husband concerning family matters. This requires open discussion and much prayer. This is not the time to close down or minimize communication since your united front will help to bring a peaceful resolution to difficult experiences. Seeking the Lord together (this may be awkward at first) will give you answers as to how to respond, react, and relate to the things that your child has shared with you.

It is also vital that you let your husband and children know that you love them unconditionally, right where they are at this particular point in their lives. Your husband may doubt his abilities to lead the family. Your support will assure him that he is up to the task. He needs support without criticism. He needs to know that even though you both have not been perfect parents up to this point (no one is), it is possible to follow God's plan from this point forward.

Letting your child know that he or she is always accepted (even though the lifestyle choices may not be) and that you want to maintain the relationship with them can be very free-ing for them. Your child may still decide to walk away or sever the relationship. However, knowing that, like the prodigal son, he can always come home may be pivotal for his walk into freedom.

It is crucial to examine yourself, much like husbands have been encouraged to do. How have you been responding to your family members? Have you allowed your husband to take his place in the home, or have you tried to lead the family your-self? Have you been overbearing or smothering toward your children? Have you treated your children without favoritism? Have you encouraged and supported your children according to their individual personalities and talents without comparing them to their siblings? Have you allowed depression or self-doubt to limit your ability to parent? And very importantly, do you pray daily for your husband and children? Prayer is often the greatest weapon we have in tackling hardships.

Asking yourself some of these questions may be painful and the answers hard to accept. The flip side of this, however, is that change in our families will always start with ourselves. We should never underestimate the positive impact that our change can have on their lives.

In conclusion, Peter gives husbands and wives a strong framework for the marriage relationships. "Finally, all of you should be of one mind. Sympathize with each other. Love each other as brothers and sisters. Be tenderhearted, and keep a humble attitude. Don't repay evil for evil. Don't retaliate with insults when people insult you. Instead, pay them back with a blessing. That is what God has called you to do, and he will grant you his blessing" (1 Peter 3:8-9, NLT). If we would simply model this way of life in our homes, then many of the problems we face would be diminished. These verses set a high standard, but it is time for all of us to weave the Word of God into our daily lives as we become "doers of the word and not merely hearers who delude themselves" (James 1:22, NASB).

Here are a few more scriptures for marriage:

- Genesis 2:24
- Proverbs 18:22
- Ecclesiastes 4:12
- 1 Corinthians 13:4-7
- Ephesians 5:22-33
- Hebrews 13:4

| Part 3 |

THE PARENTS

Chapter 8

VALIDATING WITHOUT CELEBRATING

People want to be validated. They may not always know what they are looking for or perhaps can't put it into words, but that is what they seek from each other and from God. God created us with a need to be loved and valued. Merriam-Webster defines value as, "relative worth, merit, or importance." To validate someone is to "make valid, substantiate, confirm." Another way to say it is, "to give official sanction, confirmation, or approval to" ("value," Merriam-Webster).

It has been said that a child's validation comes from the father and the mother does the nurturing. There is a big difference between acknowledging our children's accomplishments and validating their very presence in the world. Our children, regardless of anything else at this point, should know that we love them just because they are our children.

If the validation process is interrupted or non-existent when a child is young, they often seek approval from other sources. Though there are a number of reasons why a young person starts experiencing same-sex attraction, a common thread seems to be the absence of a healthy relationship with at least one parent. This is not always the case, however. Some children have wonderful relationships with their Christian parents, yet they choose to go their own way.

If, however, there is an absent father, an abusive father (physically or emotionally), or an alcoholic father, then a son will look for male approval from other sources. He might form a healthy relationship with a grandfather, uncle, or other male role model; but, in some cases, he will seek that attention and approval from another male peer. This may be a time in his life when he could become attracted to a homosexual relationship. The desire to be validated and loved is a powerful need.

People who are insecure want to be validated—valued and loved. When our children are not validated, they can display a sense of low self-esteem and a lack of self-confidence. Unfortunately, many children do not realize just how much God loves them. "Do not be afraid, for I have ransomed you. I have called you by name; you are mine" (Isaiah 43:1, NLT).

When your children go to their peers, family members, or especially you as a parent, they want affirmation, approval, and acceptance regarding their lifestyle choice. They want their lifestyle choice and partner to be accepted by everyone as well, and continue to be allowed into the family and all other relationships.

Christian parents ultimately struggle with trying to validate their children, but not their choices—especially those that go against the Word of God. God's laws transcend time and culture. It becomes critical at this point that as parents, we understand that we are bound by our covenant relationship with God to please God and not man. We need to be careful that we don't conform to worldly standards just because other parents may do so. Romans 12:2 says, "Don't copy the behavior and customs of this world, but let God transform you into a new person by changing the way you think. Then you will learn to know God's will for you, which is good and pleasing and perfect"(NLT).

We validate our children because of who they are, not because of their actions or lifestyle choices. Psalm 127:3 says, "Children are a gift from the LORD; they are a reward from him" (NLT). Often, when parents see a child through the label "gay," they forget to see their child's goals, talents, and accomplishments. That should not be so.

A gay child will often tell the parent, "If you love me, you will support me for who I am!" At this point, the child wants the parent to validate lifestyle choices. We still love our children, but we need to understand that their choices have now become their own, and the consequences can be devastating. Parents must not validate sinful choices in any area of life.

Have a discussion as soon as you can with your child about what you believe and why. You may need to do some research and ask yourself, "What exactly do I believe?" You must be able to back up what you believe with Scripture. Consider passages such as Leviticus 18:22, Romans 1:24-32, Jude 7:8, 1 Corinthians 6:9-11, Genesis 1:26-28, 2:18-24, 1 Timothy 1:8-11, and finally, Hebrews 13:4.

As parents, we love our children and want the very best for them. We are often willing to do anything to see them grow up with better lives than we had. We want them to live out their dreams and will try to help them in any way we can.

Unconditional love is what you and I receive from God, in spite of our choices and mistakes. As a parent, relative, or friend of someone struggling with same-sex attraction, our love must be unconditional; it must never waver or be questioned. Roman 2:4 says, "Don't you see how wonderfully kind, tolerant, and patient God is with you? Does this mean nothing to you? Can't you see that His kindness is intended to turn you from your sin" (NLT).

Compassion without compromise is being kindhearted without discounting the Word of God. Assure your child of your love and that you will not disown, reject, or throw him out. However, see that God's truth and righteousness prevail. We need to help children see that they are not being rejected. We do not want them to feel alone or like strangers or outsiders.

| Chapter 9 |

ESTABLISHING BOUNDARIES

A host of issues arise after a friend, child, or other family member enters a same-sex relationship. Suddenly you are confronted with situations you have never had to deal with before. Parents who have a child in a homosexual relationship need wisdom in setting boundaries. Do you allow his partner into your home? Do you attend a same-sex wedding of a friend or family member? Is it alright to visit with them in a neutral place? How do you handle holidays? Addressing these questions requires wisdom, love, and godly courage. You must be led by the Holy Spirit and Scripture to deal with these topics.

I can provide direction from what I have learned when counseling parents who have had to make these decisions. However, you need to make your own personal choices in these matters. As parents, your number-one priority is to act and speak in a manner that is pleasing to God. When you respond in a way that honors God's Word, you give Him authority and control over the situation. That doesn't mean you will see immediate results in your loved one when you take a biblical position. In fact, you might be confronted with anger from the person with whom you are setting boundaries.

Let's look at a few of the possible scenarios that may arise. Parents are the gatekeepers of the home, determining what is and is not allowed there. So what do you do when your child or other family member desires to bring a partner into your home for a visit or to share a holiday? If the person is your son or daughter and they are still living in your home, then I would not allow a partner to visit. To do so would put your stamp of approval on the relationship, even if that is not your intention. Most certainly, I would not let the partner spend the night. What if you, as a married person, brought someone into your home with whom you were having an affair? I am sure your child, most likely, would not approve of the relationship and would not want that to occur. Both of these relationships, an affair and a homosexual relationship, are not biblically acceptable. In addition, you need to ask yourself what affect allowing this same-sex relationship may have on your other children who remain in the home.

That does not mean that your child's partner should be treated with disdain or hate. The people involved are of great value, but the relationship is not scriptural. You may feel that you can visit outside of your home at a more neutral location. The important thing is that you keep the relationship with your loved one as strong as possible, even though you have a major disagreement with their lifestyle choice. You want to have a godly influence because you love your child and are concerned for her spiritual welfare. Quality time is necessary to make that happen. Therefore, you might want to spend time together eating dinner at a restaurant or at some other enjoyable location.

If your child invited you to their home for dinner or simply to visit and their partner is also present, accept the invitation. Jesus sat down and ate with sinners many times: "Levi invited Jesus and his disciples to his home as dinner guests, along with many tax collectors and other disreputable sinners" (Mark 2:15, NLT). His goal was clear, however. He influenced their lives during the process and not vice versa.

What if your child is older and does not live at home? It goes without saying that you should let your child visit without the partner. But, what about a visit from both of them? I, personally, do not feel it is appropriate to have a homosexual couple, whether it is my child or not, come into my home. My question is, will they respect my boundaries? I would like to think they would, but from my own experience, I didn't, my brother didn't, and they probably won't either. I know this is a tricky issue. You must be led by the Spirit here. All children should be welcomed to come home.

If you are invited to a same-sex wedding, only you can decide whether or not to attend. But let's clarify something right now; it is not a marriage, only a civil union. Remember, marriage was designed by God to be between one man and one woman. Emotionally, this is an extremely difficult decision, especially if the ceremony is for your child. Having said that, to participate in the civil union of a same-sex couple would be a violation of Scripture. I believe that your mere presence at the ceremony indicates your support for the homosexual union. You have been invited to participate in the celebration of a union that is against God's plan and is a challenge to your values.

As a person who believes what the Bible says regarding homosexuality, I could not attend a same-sex union. Is it possible to express your love to your child and at the same time not attend? Yes, instead of giving a gift or celebratory card, thank him/her for the invitation and respectfully decline the offer. Then you can go on to explain that although you love him/her very much, you cannot support a marriage that was not designed by God.

You should always let your children know that you will be praying for them. We always hope that our sons and daughters will understand and accept our values. However, that may not always be the case.

A dear friend of mine recently had to follow this principle when his child decided to enter into a same-sex union. The day of the event, instead of attending the ceremony, the family came together, had a meal, and prayed for their child. They did not waver in their decision to not attend the union but went a step further, joining forces with family members to intercede on their child's behalf.

The same-sex couple will probably not accept or agree with your decision, and there's a very real possibility that they will become quite angry. Sometimes the pressure becomes so heavy that many parents give in and compromise on the core beliefs they have learned from Scripture. Remember, you must have compassion without compromising the gospel. Politically correct bashing from society will often come, some of it from other family members and friends. You will be "persecuted for believing God's word" (Mark 4:17, NLT).

Persecution is difficult for any of us to face. When it comes from our own family members, it can be heartbreaking. The coercion and even intimidation to approve and celebrate homosexuality has never been greater. Even when you express your faith and beliefs in a respectful, loving way, you still may be the recipient of negative attacks. Name calling and insults will most likely come your way.

Jesus said in John 15:20, "Since they persecuted me, naturally they will persecute you" (NLT). Jesus never sinned or caused harm to anyone, yet He was attacked and eventually executed. A Bible promise that we don't often like to claim is found in 2 Timothy 3:12 which says, "Yes, and everyone who wants to live a godly life in Christ Jesus will suffer persecution" (NLT). There is something about a light shining in dark places. Thankfully, not everyone who is presented with the gospel persecutes the messenger. Many will eventually accept it as the Holy Spirit works in their heart. But we must be steadfast in spite of all persecution that comes our way.

In Mark 4, Jesus said that when persecution arises, some people will forsake the Word that is sown in their hearts. We see this happening with many people—including parents. Even some churches have changed their statement of beliefs to appease society. Preparation is vital if you are going to withstand persecution as it starts to escalate. First, keep your relationship with God front and center; continue to fellowship with Him in prayer and Bible reading each day. If you're not being spiritually fed and watered, then you will not stand when the wind and waves come against you. Are you consistently studying the Word? Be sure to spend time daily communing with God so that when those difficult times come, you are already growing in a relationship with Him.

Second, attach yourself to a church with sound biblical doctrine, and also get involved in a small group within a body of believers. It can be a group specifically for men, women, married couples, or some other kind of Bible study. Getting involved in these groups will provide strength and comfort for you during hard times. There are many churches out there, so take a look at their vision and mission statement to see what their church doctrine is regarding marriage. Especially look to find their stand on homosexuality. I would suggest you meet with the pastor of the church and bring your questions to him about what the church believes.

Finally, take advantage of Christian organizations that speak to the issue of homosexuality. Growing in knowledge on this topic is so important. These organizations can share with you their experiences and resources as well as offer prayer support. There are many resources available; a list of some ministries can be found at the back of this book. Please use the resources available to you.

There are many decisions, some of them extremely difficult, that you and your family are going to have to make as a result of your child's lifestyle choice. Please understand that the underlying principle that should guide you is what we call "compassion without compromise." You want to be kind, loving, and respectful to your loved ones and their friends who are struggling with same-sex attraction. At the same time, you do not want to affirm their lifestyle choice or advance any initiative of the gay political movement.

| Chapter 10 |

Parents Persevere

This is the day and time when parents need to stand strong and not give up or become discouraged. One of the greatest tools the enemy uses is discouragement. "This is my command—be strong and courageous! Do not be afraid or discouraged. For the LORD your God is with you wherever you go" (Joshua 1:9, NLT). If we relax our hold on what we know through God's Word to be true and right, the enemy has an opportunity to gain a foothold in our lives. If we give up on our hope in the Lord and the promises He offers in His Word, the enemy has gained the upper hand.

I know of a sweet 80-year-old woman whose son is still in the homosexual lifestyle. She has stayed faithful for over 30 years, trusting her son will leave the lifestyle. She may not live to see it happen, but like Abraham, she is trusting faithfully. We may not see the answer to all of our prayers, but we must *never* stop believing and having faith.

We always can look to Jesus as our example. In Luke, He told His disciples a parable to the effect that they should always pray and never lose heart or give up (Luke 18:1). The parable was about a widow who went before a judge and asked him to protect, defend, and give her justice against her enemy. At first, the judge didn't want to give her the time of day. Yet because she continued to persevere, he provided her with the assistance she needed. Jesus went on to ask His disciples a couple of questions: Will not our just God defend and protect and avenge His chosen ones? When the Son of Man comes, will He find persistence in faith on the earth? In other words, are we able to trust God to come through for us, even in our darkest times? Are we willing to stand and believe until we see the results? In Ephesians 6:13, Paul encourages us, "Therefore, put on every piece of God's armor so you will be able to resist the enemy in the time of evil. Then after the battle you will still be standing firm" (NLT).

There are many great examples of men and women in the Bible who were given a vision by God and had to believe Him that it would come to pass, even against insurmountable odds. Abraham was told by God that He would make of him a great nation; that his descendants would be as many as the stars if they were able to be counted. God spoke to Abraham and said that in him would all the families and kindred of the earth be blessed. This was a terrific promise, but Abraham did not see the start of this promise being fulfilled until he was 100 years old. Nevertheless, the Bible tells us in Genesis 15:6 that he believed in, trusted in, relied on, and remained steadfast in what God had spoken to him. This was why the promise of a great nation was fulfilled.

In the book of Exodus, Moses was given the task of leading the people of Israel out of bondage from Egypt. This particular challenge seemed daunting and impossible to both

Moses and his brother, Aaron, who had been appointed to be his spokesman and helper. Indeed, they not only had to go up against the Israelites who complained about the process, but also against a very stubborn Pharaoh. But God was faithful to fulfill His promise to lead the Israelites into their promised land and the people were able to dance and sing before Him, "For He has triumphed gloriously; he has hurled both horse and rider into the sea" (Exodus 15:21, NLT).

There will be times of discouragement. Let's not kid ourselves about that. It is hard to stand firm on a daily basis. But God and His Word will be your stability in the difficult times. The Holy Spirit is called our Comforter. He's the One called alongside to help us when all we can see with our natural eyes is a negative situation (see John 14:16).

Another thing that will be very helpful in your quest to remain faithful to the calling of God is to remember that He has never given up on you. No matter how distant you once were from Him, or how many times you have "blown it," He has continued to reach out His hand of grace and called you closer to Himself. The Father does not say, "This is too hard; it is taking too long; and the people are too stubborn." We can be thankful for His patience and that His mercies are new every morning. That is why we should never give up on ourselves while we are becoming everything we were intended to be, and why we should not give up on others who are on their journey toward wholeness.

Determine these things in your mind:

- We will not give up when we do not see immediate results for what we are longing for in our lives and in the lives of our loved ones.
- We will not give up when we are feeling disappointed and/or tired of waiting for the good results.
- We will not give up under mounting pressure. This pressure can be from society, the media, or simply from those around us who say we must be culturally relevant.
- We will not give up when every circumstance we observe looks bleak.

When you make the determination to follow the path God has called you to:

- Never stop praying and standing for what is right.
- Never stop believing for the best in your loved ones.
- Never stop seeking God if you are struggling.

Remember the words of Galatians 6:9-10: "So let's not get tired of doing what is good. At just the right time we will reap a harvest of blessing if we don't give up. Therefore, whenever we have the opportunity, we should do good to everyone—especially to those in the family of faith" (NLT).

A Special Word to Parents in Ministry

Many people wonder what they should do when they have raised their child in the nurture and admonition of the Lord, and the child chooses to walk a path that is contrary to what they know is right. Parents in this situation who are also in the ministry may feel they are no longer qualified to continue with the calling God has given them. Though they attempt to reach out to others, they wonder about their ability to continue to do so when their own child has walked away from godly values. How do these parents continue to stand for truth when modern culture says they should just "live and let live"?

Others may become disheartened because though they have chosen to walk in righteousness, they have fallen into temptation. They may have bought into the lie that they are no longer good enough to earn God's love or that they have gone too far to turn back.

Each one of us has been given a call, a vision, to walk in right standing with God and also to be used by Him to let His light shine in a dark world. Even though we sometimes question whether we can continue to carry out the ministry God has called us to, we must not let Satan discourage us or cause us to let go of that calling.

Proverbs 29:18 says, "Where there is no vision [no redemptive revelation of God], the people perish" (AMP). This is the point where we need to keep the vision we have been given before our eyes. In Habakkuk 2:2-3, we are encouraged to write the vision clearly, and even if it tarries, we wait for it earnestly because it will surely come to fruition.

The darkness all around us often leaves us feeling like salmon swimming upstream trying to reach our intended destination. Miraculously, salmon do reach their destination, and we too can see our vision realized. It is the supernatural power of God at work in us that causes this to happen. He uses ordinary people to accomplish the work that needs to be done on this earth. This has never been truer than in present times. It is exciting when we realize that we can be bearers of light in a dark world. Isaiah 9:2 says, "The people who walk in darkness have seen a great Light; those who dwelt in the land of intense darkness and the shadow of death, upon them has the Light shined" (AMP).

If you are a parent who has been called to minister to others, please continue to pursue that calling. Continue to persevere and believe that God will deliver your children out of the homosexual lifestyle. God will use you regardless of your past, what your children are doing, or any doubt the enemy may throw your way. Stand firm. God's Word promises that if we stay steadfast on the course, we will see victory. And all the glory will go to God!

| Chapter 11 |

WORKING THROUGH GRIEF

I t can hit you like a punch in the gut. Your son or daughter just told you that he or she is gay. Some cultures address the issue of homosexuality differently than other cultures. From the experience of our ministry, every parent is going to respond to this issue differently.

It is important to understand that you will most likely go through some or all of the stages of grief (denial, anger, bargaining, depression, and acceptance) as you come to terms with what has taken place. These stages are normal. However, you must pass through them in a healthy way in order to take appropriate action and be in a position to be used by God to influence your child in a positive way.

Many children are deeply hurt when their parents respond to their admission with an attitude of denial. In essence, the parent is telling the child that the same-sex attraction they're experiencing is not real. This parental reaction—and it is a reaction—only serves to frustrate the child and may potentially put an abrupt end to any further disclosures.

Communication is paramount. As parents, we must resist the urge to say things like, "You were raised as a Christian, so you can't be experiencing these feelings. You're just confused right now, you'll get over it. That's just silly and ridiculous."

Some parents simply ignore what their child discloses, hoping it will all just go away. What we often do not realize is that the child probably has experienced years of lonely heartache trying to deal with these unwanted feelings and attractions. They have cried many tears of anguish. It took a lot of courage for the child to address the subject with the parents, so we must not lightly dismiss him with a superficial answer that appears to be a brush-off. Instead, at this critical moment of disclosure, we need to be able to somehow affirm the son or daughter and the courage it took for them to open up. But in doing this, parents must not show acceptance for the homosexual lifestyle.

At the moment feelings of same-sex attraction are revealed by the child, he or she needs understanding and empathy instead of a "quick fix" response. Keep in mind Hebrews 4:15 (NLT) which says, "This High Priest of ours understands our weaknesses, for he faced all of the same testings we do, yet he did not sin." Jesus sympathizes and has compassion toward us in the midst of our temptations. In the same way, our love must always be evident without condoning the sin. If a child cannot sense our love for him or her, then he or she is unlikely to receive any counsel or direction that we may provide.

Christian parents may find it more difficult to believe that their child is dealing with same-sex attraction than non-Christians. After all, you have read your child Bible stories from the time he was born, taken him to church each week, sent him to a Christian school, signed him up for church camp each year, and endeavored to set a good example for him. So it's understandable that your first reaction is unbelief or denial. It just seems too difficult for you to comprehend.

Sometimes we mistakenly think that our children will not be tempted with the same things as those "in the world." But we must be alert to the enemy's tactics. When we see a "red flag" in our child's behavior or when something unusual is said, we need to pause and pray about exploring the matter instead of ignoring the warning signs. Think about how the enemy schemed to murder Jesus when He was born. Herod, who was under demonic influence to stop the plan of man's redemption, went to extreme lengths and ordered all of the babies murdered who were two years old and under. Therefore, our own children, the ones who are the dearest to our hearts, also will be the target of the enemy.

The Bible speaks of the fallen world we live in, and it's interesting to observe how the world's system is attempting to take more and more control of our children's lives. The things taught in schools regarding sexuality are a case in point. It appears that the goal of some of the curriculum is to mold the moral beliefs of our children and give them choices for sexual behaviors that are *not* based on God's word. There is a battle raging against our families, and we must protect our children! Parents must have an ongoing dialogue with their children to keep the doors of communication open.

Be careful not to resort to anger. An angry response often drives a wedge between parents and their child. For example, a college-aged daughter just informed her parents she is gay. Her parents rush into action and take away their daughter's car and financial support for her education. This harsh response, or one similar, happens quite often. The parents' response was motivated out of the anger and hurt they were feeling at the moment. Such actions have the appearance of a bribe or manipulation to coerce the son or daughter into forsaking the lifestyle. The result, however, is rarely positive. An angry response neglects the deeper questions that should be explored to try to find out why the child believes she is gay.

There are many reasons why a son or daughter feels drawn to the lifestyle. It could be a poor relationship with a parent(s), lack of a parent, bullying suffered at the hands of peers, sexual abuse, or a traumatic experience. It also could be that they simply need to overcome their fallen nature by walking in the light of God's Word and Spirit. With prayer and godly counsel, attempt to respond to your child in an effort to help, instead in an initial reflex of anger.

Many parents and grandparents struggle with feeling like a dark cloud is hanging over their heads. Feelings of heaviness and depression often descend following a child's revelation of being gay. Parents engage in a great deal of introspection to determine where they have failed in raising their child. This is especially true of parents who have made it their goal to live as a Christ-centered family, based on God's Word. This is an important stage that must be worked through.

Yes, it's true that we must allow the Lord to search our hearts to determine what shortcomings may have existed in our parental skills and philosophy. Did some of our actions contribute to this situation and our child's self-identity? There are no perfect parents. We have all fallen short. Abuse, whether physical, emotional, or sexual would obviously have serious consequences. It's amazing how many times the revelation of sexual abuse inflicted by someone close to the family comes to light after hours of trying to figure out what could have gone wrong in their child. There are no perfect parents. We have all fallen short. Professional counseling will most likely be needed in this case, as well as legal action.

In other situations, one or both parents may need to repent and possibly ask forgiveness from their child because of poor decisions. Forcing a child to play sports instead of engaging in the arts or vice versa, putting down and belittling a child, making unkind remarks about the child's appearance, being insensitive to the fragility of their self-esteem, failure to identify bullying at school, and a myriad of other offenses may need to be forgiven. Once they have asked for forgiveness, the parents must move beyond their feelings of guilt and failure by receiving God's forgiveness and then forgiving themselves.

In the final analysis, this is a choice the child has made. Don't constantly dwell on all the things you may have done wrong. The tendency for some parents is to overly examine every little thing that they may have done incorrectly. We cannot engage in this type of thinking because it tends to bring our own lives to a screeching halt to the point where we are never able to move on.

God wants you to move forward and serve Him with an even greater fervency, not shrink back from your service to Him. If you want to be in a strong spiritual position to be able to help your child, then you must forget what lies behind and look forward to what lies ahead (Philippians 3:13). Remember the prodigal son's father was ready for the return of his son. His desire to see his son well caused him to respond correctly and in a godly manner when the son returned.

As a parent, you must get over the temptation to become storm-tossed by every negative wave that breaks over your life. We cannot live by what we see or hear; we have to have faith in God that He is working in our children's lives. Fear and worry will leave us exhausted and defeated. They leave us paralyzed. Put your son or daughter in God's hands, and thank God right now, even if you do not see any positive signs that they are responding. Seek support from trustworthy sources. You will realize there are many parents experiencing the same situation as you.

There is another area that you should keep in mind. The upheaval that accompanies dealing with the issues unique to having a gay son or daughter can manifest itself in your marriage. Finger-pointing and division are very real pitfalls. Out of a heart of hurt, frustration, and pain, a spouse might blame the partner for what is taking place. This will not be helpful. On the contrary, it stops real progress and healing. You may have other children in the home who need you. Don't be sidetracked by mudslinging. Each partner should search his own heart to find out if changes are necessary. Bringing in a pastor or counselor might be advisable to help work through some of these issues.

Keep the goal before you—the spiritual well-being of your child—instead of the faults of each other. In many cases, neither partner is at fault. Husbands and wives should put a priority on their relationship. Invest in it. Go on a date regularly. This is a time to pull together. Pray together, forgive each other, and seek out information that will encourage and strengthen your relationship. Attend church. If ministries offer classes for marriage support or men and women's topics, take advantage of them. As a couple, get involved serving in a ministry at your church. In other words, consider your marriage as a top priority in your lives. If you are not married, please seek help and encouragement from godly people and your church.

C. S. Lewis said, "No one ever told me grief felt so much like fear." Grief often creeps in, and before you know it, you find yourself disappointed not only in your children, but in life in general. The idea of moving to the final stage of grief, acceptance, can seem like an impossible endeavor.

While we shouldn't deny that our child is having these feelings and struggles, we should not accept that this is the end of their story. Even if everything looks bleak and they are resistant to everything you hold dear, you should not throw up your hands in surrender. In the beginning, God did not accept the fact that Adam and Eve doomed everyone for eternity. Instead, God immediately set a plan for redemption into motion. Parents and loved ones, after having done all to stand, stand (Ephesians 6:13-14).

So, my dear brothers and sisters, be strong and immovable. Always work enthusiastically for the Lord, for you know that nothing you do for the Lord is ever useless.

1 CORINTHIANS 15:58 NLT

| Chapter 12 |

Praying Effectively

I t is never an easy thing to hear that your child has chosen the gay lifestyle. This will become a time of reflection as a parent. The first question you will probably ask yourself is, "What did I do wrong?" The question also needs to be asked, "What did I do right?" The enemy would like you to take the blame for your child's decision. However, this does not allow our children to take responsibility for their own decisions. A person cannot acknowledge sin without accepting responsibility.

As parents, we need to seek out God's counsel. Ask God to reveal any area of parenting where you need to seek forgiveness from God, your child and yourself. It is a true act of humility and love to recognize that there may have been areas where we let our children down—not enough time spent with them, inability to connect with them, not listening to them, exposing them to things that were dangerous or unhealthy. The list could be endless, but everything on it is always forgivable. Repentance on our part can establish a foundation of love and forgiveness in the relationship with our child. Once we have repented, it is time to take action. And that always starts with prayer.

Pray without ceasing, trusting and believing God can and will set your child free.

- Pray that your child pursues God (Hosea 2:14-15).

- Pray that God will send people into your child's life who will speak love and acceptance.

- Pray that your child will be exposed to the gospel. God may use a way or means you do not understand. Remember, God is in control, not you.

- Pray that your heart will stay soft and open to your child. Remember, when God calls out, He calls out in love.

- Pray for healing of past emotions, trauma, loneliness, rejection, and insecurities.

- Pray that your child embraces a fear of the Lord and a reverence for God. Rebellion becomes a way of life when our children lose their fear of the Lord.

- Pray that the goodness of God will draw your child near to repentance—not the fear of judgment from God or man, but love— pure love.

- Pray for your child's future spouse.

- Pray for your child's future children.
- Pray for your child's future ministries.
- Pray what isn't as if it already was.
- Pray for creative miracles. There is no limit to what God can do.
- Pray that your child becomes sensitive to the voice of God.
- Pray that your child has not given away his or her salvation. It wasn't God's will for your child to be gay. We have free will.
- Pray for understanding that the void created in your child's life through sin can only be filled by and with God.
- Pray prayers that God can agree with.
- Pray that your child's heart remains soft and does not become hardened.
- Pray that your child's eyes would be opened to the destructive consequences of his or her choices.
- Pray that your child will live the life that God purposed for him or her from the beginning of time.

Stay alert! Watch out for your great enemy, the devil. He prowls around like a roaring lion, looking for someone to devour.

1 PETER 5:8 NLT

Never stop praying. Be thankful in all circumstances, for this is God's will for you who belong to Christ Jesus.

1 THESSALONIANS 5:17-18 NLT

Faith is the confidence that what we hope for will actually happen; it gives us assurance about things we cannot see.

HEBREWS 11:1 NLT

Pray in faith. Cover your children daily in prayer. Don't ever give up because of what you see, but persevere because of what you know of God's character. Stand on His Word and His promises. God does not lie. Remember these words from the book of Romans:

And I am convinced that nothing can ever separate us from God's love. Neither death nor life, neither angels nor demons, neither our fears for today nor our worries about tomorrow—not even the powers of hell can separate us from God's love. No power in the sky above or in the earth below—indeed, nothing in all creation will ever be able to separate us from the love of God that is revealed in Christ Jesus our Lord.

ROMANS 8:38-39 NLT

I would like to end this section with a prayer by Amy Carmichael, a missionary to India for over 50 years. She worked with the children who were sold into sexual slavery.

Prayer for Children

Father, hear us, we are praying.
Hear the words our hearts are saying.
We are praying for our children.
Keep them from the powers of evil,
From the secret, hidden perils,
From the whirlpool that would suck them,
From the treacherous quicksand pluck them.
From the world's hollow gladness,
From the sting of faithless sadness,
Holy Father, save our children.
Through life's troubled waters steer them,
Through life's bitter battle, cheer them,
Father, Father, be thou near them.
Read the language of our longing,
Read the wordless pleadings thronging,
Holy Father for our children,
And wherever they may abide,
Lead them home at eventide.

Part 4

GENDER CONFUSION

Chapter 13

MY STORY
BY WALT HEYER

I have been a part of the transgender world on some level now for 70 years.

It started at the tender age of four with the assistance and encouragement of my grandma to cross-dress in the rundown house behind an auto junkyard she shared with my grandpa. I was a small, slender young boy. Grandma made me a purple chiffon evening dress to wear during our secret play time. The scene is seared in my memory: me modeling the soft flowing dress standing on a footstool and reveling in her words of affirmation and smiles of praise. To this day, I remember how much better she enjoyed me as a little girl. Like all children, I thrived on the positive attention. She never made a fuss over me as a boy, but she sure loved me as a little girl. Her affirmation and assistance in cross-dressing me affected my life deeply because it happened so early in life. It led to the development of psychological disorders, which were undiagnosed and untreated and ultimately turned my life upside down.

When my parents eventually found out about my wearing girls' clothes at Grandma's, they were appalled and never let me stay alone at Grandma's again. My mom and dad were good parents. My mom worked in a clothing factory and married my dad at the age of 18. Dad was tough, kind, and smart, a hard-working "man's man." My dressing up as a little girl was very troubling to him, especially considering it was the mid-1940s. But looking like a girl became part of who I was.

The discovery of the cross-dressing set off a chain of unpleasant events. I suspect both Dad and Mom became more aggressive with discipline out of frustration with me. My dad's adopted brother, himself only a teenager, began to tease and make fun of me when he found out I had cross-dressed. Later, when I was about eight years old, he molested me several times. My gender confusion never went away and grew even stronger over time. I continued to cross-dress in adulthood, even though I was married with children, but I never cross-dressed in the family home. I felt that would be too psychologically damaging to my children. As time went on, I wanted to change genders. I was divorced prior to my reassignment surgery.

In 1983 at the age of 42, I sought approval for, and underwent, gender reassignment surgery. My approval for surgery came from the highest authority on the subject, the very man who authored the first edition of *The Harry Benjamin International Standards of Care* for treating transgenders, Dr. Paul Walker. The surgeon who performed my gender reassignment surgery, Dr. Stanley Biber, was the premier surgeon in the U.S. for that type of surgery. The two premier authorities on gender reassignment at the time determined my treatment plan.

I legally changed my birth record from Walt Heyer, male, to Laura Jensen, female, and successfully worked and lived as a female for eight years. But I still was troubled and anxious, even after gender reassignment and years of living as female. The first years after surgery went well. But when I realized eight years later that the surgical change was incapable of biologically changing a man into a woman, I was troubled by the fraud of a gender change. I embarked on a study of psychology and discovered among the pages of the psychology books, disorders I never knew existed. I learned that psychological disorders can develop over time, and they can cause the feelings of wanting to be the other gender.

Separation anxiety disorder was the first disorder to resonate with me. It usually means a psychological condition where depression and anxiety can cause a child to become fearful and filled with nervous anxiety when away from home. In my case, it was fear of what my mom or dad would do when they discovered the secret at Grandma's house. In my psychology class, I learned of other disorders such as dissociative disorders, where the person does not want to be who he is because of unhealthy and unpleasant events that occurred early in life. The traumatic events can include the death of a parent, sexual abuse, divorce, alcoholism, or mental illness in the home. One or both parents may have physically abandoned the family or been simply emotionally unavailable.

When I learned this, I was 50 years old. Forty-six years had passed since my first cross-dressing episode. I hadn't considered that the abuse in my childhood—Grandma's cross-dressing of me, the heavy discipline from my parents and the molesting by my uncle—could cause mental disorders. All I knew was that I was driven by feelings to change genders. It is difficult to pull apart strong feelings as an adult and link them to long-buried childhood memories. I didn't talk about the hurt; it remained locked up inside. The early cross-dressing did not seem harmful at the time, but as I started to look back from the vantage point of my 50s, I could see it had turned from what was fun for me and my grandma to years of unfortunate consequences, pain, and the loss of a boy's childhood innocence. After eight years of living as a woman, expressing myself as the opposite gender was not relieving my anxiety any more, but rather, seemed to be fueling it. The more I learned about the psychological implications of my early life, the more I became determined to overcome my horrible start to life. I may have had a rough start, but I wanted to finish life well.

For me, psychotherapy was the treatment I chose to deal with the feelings that started so early in life. I went to a therapist three times a week. Eventually, through psychotherapy and months that turned into years of hard work, I was able to resolve my twisted concept of who I was and who I had become. I healed from the past and no longer felt the need to live as a trans-woman. I transitioned back in 1994 and fully recovered. Now, I am a happily married man of 18 years, and I have no need to go back to the trans-madness ever again. As best I can, I attempt to tell my story in hopes of preventing someone else from an unnecessary gender change that can end in regret, or worse, suicide.

Ten years ago, I set up a website, www.sexchangeregret .com, to share my journey and reach out to others. As a result, I hear from people who write to me with their own stories of gender transition and de-transition. I have had the benefit of learning that regret is not rare at all; it is quite common but only comes to light later, after the initial euphoria wears off. I've heard from people from three weeks to 30 years post-gender reassignment who want to know how to de-transition.

Other things I've learned include:

- According to research studies, 62.7 percent of transgenders are suffering from undiagnosed and untreated comorbid disorders.
- Proof of regret is the reason for the alarmingly high attempted suicide rate for transgenders: over 50 percent for ages 10 to 24 and 41 percent for those 25 and up.
- Another unfortunate reality is that, according to studies, transgenders are 49 times more likely to contract AIDS.

People who enjoy their life do not attempt suicide. If life as the opposite gender were good, transgenders would not be attempting suicide at such a high rate. I hope that people who read this will see that caution is required, not condemnation. Proceed slowly and consider this: feelings, even strong ones, change over time.

For more information, please visit my website at www.waltheyer.com.

Chapter 14

Q & A on Transgender Issues

with Walt Heyer

1. How can a parent pray effectively for a child who is cross-dressing and/or transitioning?

Parents, pray for guidance from the Lord in providing a safe, loving home for your children. Pray God's Word over their lives (Ephesians 3:14-20).

2. How should parents talk to their child about this without fear that he will lose his cool or take it personally?

Parents must be vigilant in verbally affirming the child in positive ways. Parents must take time to listen to their child and (calmly) ask why they want to change genders. This is usually a point of discovery for the parents.

My life as a four-year-old boy provides all the evidence we need to see how trans-kids are shaped from their experiences with adults (or lack of adults) during the early developmental years. Kids learn and develop self-identity and gender identity from the people who talk, walk, and play with them. If a boy is encouraged toward manhood by a loving father, he wants to be like his dad. If he is a shy young boy, most likely he will "shy away" from dad out of fear that dad will find out what grandma has been teaching him. Sadly, now public schools are indoctrinating our children from a very young age. They are using the public school system to teach kids that homosexuality, bisexuality, and transgender behavior is normal and natural.

3. Can any of my child's behaviors be linked to me as a parent?

Children learn values, social behaviors, and belief systems from their parents. But be aware, LGBTQ activists will teach their views at school.

Parents need to consider that public schools are teaching LGBTQ gender sex values. The risk is dangerously high in keeping your children in a public school system that is largely in the hands of gay activists. But influences can also come from other places. In my case, my grandmother broke my boy identity by telling me how wonderful I looked as a girl. I felt encouraged to change genders as she repeatedly dressed me in that purple dress, and the boy in me got lost.

4. What boundaries should be set regarding wearing opposite gender clothing, etc.?

It is important to have a home where others do not encourage or celebrate cross-gender behaviors. If a child becomes involved in cross-gender behaviors, it should not be affirmed or encouraged. Doing so plants the seed of dysphoria (a confusion between the gender they were born with and the one they think they are).

Getting more "you look great" and "you are so cute" comments only fuels the desire to cross-dress. Gender dysphoria is the sign that there are underlying, untreated, and undiagnosed disorders that coexist with gender dysphoria, called "comorbid disorders." There are studies about comorbid disorders on my blog, www.waltheyer.com, which identify that 62.7 percent of transgenders have comorbid disorders. I was officially diagnosed with a "dissociative disorder," one of the many comorbid disorders that masquerade as gender dysphoria.

In 1945, when I was a child, few people knew that cross-dressing a kid would cause gender dysphoria and a life filled with pain and heartache. Today, we have no excuse. The research proves we are manufacturing transgender kids due to mandatory school reading assignments about transgenders and homosexuals. Not until President Obama set the LGBT activists loose in public schools did we ever encounter such a brazen federally-funded, homosexual agenda. Trans-kids were virtually non-existent prior to Obama's embrace of the LGBT movement.

5. How do you approach talking to your child about his feelings without shutting down open communication?

This is only a problem if the parent is being controlled by the child. Parents must start affirming the child's gender from day one. Remember, child development starts when the child comes home from the delivery room, not at four, five, or ten years of age. Parents should encourage open communication, free of anger, showing the child they are safe to talk about very difficult issues, even sexual ones.

6. What factors increase the likelihood of a person struggling with this issue?

A home life marked by:

Verbal abuse

Sexual abuse

Alcoholism and/or drug addiction

Very ill parent or parents

Divorce

Mentally ill parent(s)

A home where a suicide has occurred

A parent who has been incarcerated and otherwise unavailable

Parents who are detached from the child

A home that pushes LGBT activism (celebrates gay pride, etc.)

A home without the knowledge of the long-term devastation caused by changing genders

My home was not safe. My grandma was not safe. No place was safe from my uncle or the memories of Grandma cross-dressing me. Over and over in my head, I heard my grandma's words, "You look so nice as a girl." She never said how handsome I looked as a boy.

7. What logic, counseling, or spiritual approach has been successful in helping people reorient to accepting their God-given identity?

There is no specific guide. Each individual develops the desire to change genders because of "deep unresolved hurt." Finding the root cause of that deep hurt will help the person accept his God-given gender. It is all about the hurt.

I've come to appreciate the words of Jeremiah 1:5: "Before I shaped you in the womb, I knew all about you. Before you saw the light of day, I had holy plans for you: A prophet to the nations—that's what I had in mind for you" (MSG).

The issues kids face today are ten times more difficult than the ones I faced 70 years ago, but one thing hasn't changed. Children still do not have the benefit of sound diagnosis or treatment of the comorbid disorders (separation anxiety, post-traumatic stress, sexual abuse, PTSD, etc.) that are the cause of gender dysphoria. If they were properly diagnosed and offered effective treatment, they would no longer want to be a different gender. Today, the LGBT agenda stands in the way of anyone providing proper diagnosis and effective treatment for the psychological causes of gender dysphoria.

8. What resources are available to us as parents and to our child as he or she struggles with the transgender decision?

This is a huge problem. There are few resources and even fewer people who want to help prevent an unnecessary gender change for the age group of 10 to 24. Unfortunately, 50 percent of these people will attempt suicide. If the child says, "I will commit suicide if I do not get a gender change," you have a child who is emotionally unstable and psychologically in need of sound effective therapy. Certain states have prohibited counseling for children under 18 who struggle with sexual confusion. Counseling isn't about dictating how they should live their lives; it is a tool that will help them and the parent make educated choices in the journey they are on.

There are few people willing to step up and push back the militant LGBTQ activists. We need individuals who can offer an alternative for the future of our children.

9. What does the de-transitioning process look like?

Individuals will design their own de-transition based on surgical and hormonal requirements. Many transgenders never had bottom surgery so the physical de-transition is not complicated. Individuals who had bottom surgery will most likely not have a reversal bottom procedure because it is not functional. The details vary a great deal from one person to another because there are no required procedures, only the state requirements (different in every state) for restoring the original birth record.

| Part 5 |

THE CHURCH

Chapter 15

SEXUAL SIN IS SIN, RIGHT?

God created sex for our enjoyment. A sexual relationship is to be enjoyed within the context of a man and woman united in a marriage (covenant) relationship with God. He set this limit to protect us because when we step out of the boundary God created for sex, we step into sexual sin.

In our culture today, we are seeing a change in attitude about what constitutes sexual sin. There does not seem to be a clear definition. By that I mean that the Church does not seem to have a moral compass of what sexual sin is, let alone preach it from the pulpits, or stand up for it in the mainstream culture and media.

What about the issue of legalizing same-sex marriage? There are those who believe it can lead to other types of "marriage" relationships: an uncle and a niece, a pedophile and a child etc. I know, it all sounds far-fetched, but look where we are at today. Is it so hard to believe?

We can take this even further with the transgender movement. Will there even be a male/female gender to identify with in the next generation? The snowball starts out small but moves steadily into a full-blown avalanche in society's understanding of God's human design. We must stand up and uphold God's holy standard—sexual sin is sin!

What is going on? The enemy of our soul knows exactly what is going on; he is behind it all. What better way to deceive people than having sin not be considered an issue anymore? It exploits the grace message in that we can do what we want as Christians since there will always be God's grace. Today it appears that there is no longer any need for God's grace since there is nothing that some Christians feel we even need to be sorry for anymore.

I suppose there are many reasons why people fall into the trap of sexual sin, but simply, it is about intimacy. God wants fellowship and intimacy with man. That is why He created us. We want that with each other. False intimacy is better than no intimacy, right? Wrong! It is a spiritual issue. James 1:14-15 says, "Temptation comes from our own desires, which entice us and drag us away. These desires give birth to sinful actions. And when sin is allowed to grow, it gives birth to death" (NLT).

When our desires are to seek after God, we are on the right track. When our desires are to seek after our own selfish wants, we are led into sin. It is a serious matter, as sin keeps us from fellowship with God and potentially out of the Kingdom forever. Yes, God still loves the sinner, but only through His redemption plan are we, as sinners, able to be saved by His grace. Only then can we be in right standing with Him again.

There is a tendency in the Christian Church to focus on homosexuality as the one and only sexual sin that God judges or even pays any attention to. But the truth is homosexuality is just one of the many sexual sins listed in the Bible.

- Fornication—1 Corinthians 6:18
- Premarital Sex—Deuteronomy 22:13-21
- Bestiality—Exodus 22:19
- Adultery—Deuteronomy 5:18
- Rape—Deuteronomy 22:25-29
- Incest—Leviticus 18:6-18

God calls each and every one of us to righteousness and purity. Some churches err when they focus only on homosexuality and leave out the rest of the sexual sins. As a result, the mainstream Church is sometimes seen as unloving and harsh.

We need more courageous pastors who are willing to preach from the pulpit about sin, especially sexual sin. These are challenging times for Christians. Standing up for what is right may mean a loss of many things—our friends, our jobs, and maybe even our lives.

A tactic of the enemy is to pit churches against each other, families against families, and society against the Church. So many parents just give up and give in. Parents need to stand firm in their own lives by living a repentant and godly life. Children need the role model that God established in Leviticus and paid for on the cross. The real difficulty is helping our children to see that their sexual behavior is indeed a sin in the eyes of God. How do we do that? Hold them accountable. Don't allow the sin into your home. Don't condone their behavior. Pray that God will restore their sexual purity. Pray for a repentant heart. Remember what 2 Corinthians 12:21 says, "And I will be grieved because many of you have not given up your old sins. You have not repented of your impurity, sexual immorality, and eagerness for lustful pleasure" (NLT).

Think about this. We will be accountable for what we did and did not do here on earth. In any area of our life, not just this issue of sexual sin and homosexuality, we must walk with integrity, peace, love, and kindness. They will know that we are true Christ followers by the fruit in our lives and how we handle this controversial issue.

> Our culture has accepted two huge lies. The first is that if you disagree with someone's lifestyle, you must fear or hate them. The second is that to love someone means you agree with everything they believe or do. Both are nonsense. You don't have to compromise convictions to be compassionate.
>
> —RICK WARREN

Chapter 16

THE JUDGMENTAL CHURCH

The Church carries a heavy responsibility on the earth. It is designed to be a reflection of God to everyone who observes it. As individual Christians, we reveal Christ to those with whom we come in contact. In 2 Corinthians 5:20, we are called "ambassadors for Christ." An ambassador stands in the position of presenting the will, character, and demeanor of the person they represent. This is a sobering calling for the individual Christian and the Church as a whole. Paul says in 1 Timothy 3:15, "This is the church of the living God, which is the pillar and foundation of the truth" (NLT). Unfortunately, both the Church and individual believers have not lived up to this responsibility when it comes to our response to homosexuality. The time has come for the Church to take stock of itself and allow the Holy Spirit to transform it into the beacon of light, love, and truth that it is called to be.

It is both alarming and instructive to read about the seven churches in chapters 2-4 of the book of Revelation. Some had strayed from a pure love of God and had become self-absorbed. Jesus was calling them to return to their first love.

Our churches today, in too many cases, have lost sight of the simplicity of the gospel and instead have become more concerned with budgets, buildings, and being politically correct. Church, we must heed the same message that Jesus gave to those churches in Revelation! We must repent and then evaluate where we have drifted from loving a lost and confused world. Jesus is calling us to return to our first love and do the deeds we did when we first became believers in Christ.

New Christians seem to be always reaching out to those in the world and sharing the love of Jesus with them. Jesus showed us His priorities in the parable of the lost sheep. The Shepherd left the 99 in His fold and went out looking for the lost one. He also taught us to go out into the highways and hedges and compel the people to come to the house of God. I'll bet some of the people found in the highways and hedges were not the high society crowd. The servants who went out looking may have gotten their clothes and hands dirty in the process. In fact, Matthew 22:10 indicates that both the bad and the good were invited to the wedding feast. God's love compels us to reach out to the wise and foolish. If we are honest, we all were in the foolish category at some point in our lives.

In general, there are two wrong approaches the Church has taken toward those living a homosexual lifestyle. Some have judged and condemned the homosexual, usually in a spirit not motivated by love. Others have openly accepted the lifestyle and welcomed homosexuals into the pulpit. Both responses are ditches on the road to truth and will diminish the Church's fulfillment of its calling.

The first approach is what I call the "Sin Critical" Church. It is characterized with a primary focus on the sins and shortcomings of those outside the Church. It is quick to point out behaviors the Bible says are sinful with a harsh, condemning tone using phrases such as, "You're going to hell," "God's wrath is on you," or "God hates you." While it is true that a person living in sin and never turning from that sin to believe in the redemptive sacrifice of Jesus will not inherit the Kingdom of God (1 Corinthians 6:9), the manner in which this truth is communicated can be entirely wrong. The motivation of the person who conveys the message in this way needs to be questioned. They are not motivated by the love and grace of God, but rather, they have taken the role of a judge who has pronounced his verdict. It reminds us of how the Pharisees were always concerned with the outer appearance and actions of people, rather than the weightier spiritual needs of the individual's heart. Jesus always zoomed in on the heart. He looked beyond a person's sinfulness and invited them to follow Him.

A woman caught in the act of adultery was brought to Jesus. The scribes and Pharisees said, "The law of Moses says to stone her. What do you say?" Jesus replied, "Alright, but let the one who has never sinned throw the first stone" (John 8:4-7). Jesus was the only person who had the right to stone the woman since He was the only person without sin. Instead, He said to her, "Didn't even one of them condemn you? Neither do I. Go and sin no more." Jesus did not condone the woman's sin. Rather, He offered her forgiveness and grace.

We can look at many of Jesus' followers and discover that before coming to Christ, they lived far from saintly lives. Some had been prostitutes, swindlers and even, as we see with Paul, a murderer of innocent people.

Jesus was often accused of dining with sinners. His whole purpose on earth was to "seek and save those who are lost" (Luke 19:10). Should we, as individuals and as the Church, have a different approach to the unbeliever? I resoundingly say, "no." Should we reach out with love and forgiveness? Yes! You may ask, "What if we reach out and are rejected?" Jesus was rejected by many people but He didn't stop loving. In fact, Jesus asked the Father to forgive those who were nailing Him to the cross. Too many times we love others only when they meet our expectations. This was not and is not the attitude of Jesus.

Jesus loved us before we turned to Him. He did not say, "I will love and give My life for mankind because they are a holy and righteous people deserving of My favor." On the contrary, He loved and gave His life for us while we were still ugly and sinful. Romans 5:8 says, "But God showed His great love for us by sending Christ to die for us while we were still sinners" (NLT).

The Bible instructs us to live our lives as Jesus did (1 John 2:6). This means we must follow in His steps and love the unlovely. The title "Christian" actually means "little Christ." We must have the same attitude toward the sinner that Jesus exemplified while He walked the earth.

Again, we do not excuse or ignore sin. There is eternal punishment for the person who does not turn to Christ for redemption and forgiveness. However, the Bible states that hell was created for the devil and his angels. It was not in God's design for man to go there. But because of Adam's choice of disobedience, all of us are guilty and separated from God until we accept Jesus as our Savior. If a person does not respond to His sacrifice, then there will be a time when he will be judged. Revelation 20:11-15 tells of an impending judgment for those whose names are not written in the Book of Life.

Our mistake is that we often prematurely pass judgment. Paul said that we should not pass judgment before the appointed time (1 Corinthians 4:5). The Lord will take care of that when He returns. In the same story of the woman caught in adultery, Jesus said, "I am not judging anyone." Even though Jesus had the right to judge, He withheld doing it until the final judgment.

Sometimes in our zeal to stand up for righteousness and defend the gospel, we blur the line between the sinner and the sin itself. On one occasion, Jesus was traveling to Jerusalem and planned to stop at a village that was on His way. Jesus sent messengers ahead of Him to arrange for their stay in that village but the residents refused to accommodate them. James and John observed the villagers' negative responses and approached Jesus with a question. They asked Jesus if they should call fire down from heaven to consume those who turned them away. Jesus rebuked the two disciples and said in Luke 9:55-56, "You do not know of what sort of spirit you are, for the Son of Man did not come to destroy men's lives, but to save them [from the penalty of eternal death]" (AMP).

If James and John were not motivated by the Spirit of God, as Jesus stated, then what spirit motivated them to say what they said? The devil is the accuser. What the villagers did was wrong, and the disciples wanted them to be judged and immediately punished. Jesus' reply to His disciples is so vitally important and instructive for us. It should resonate every day in our hearts as we encounter the unsaved. Jesus came to save men, not destroy them. Like James and John, we often want to condemn those who have turned their backs on Jesus. But Jesus' whole purpose was to extend mercy and grace.

Why has Jesus not yet returned to earth? Peter said that God isn't making us wait just for the sake of waiting, but the "slowness" of His return has a definite purpose. He is being patient toward the sinner, giving them time and opportunity to repent (2 Peter 3:9).

What Peter said about the Lord's patience is important. God does not wish for any to perish. This should change our paradigm. We must not be impatient with the sinner, writing them off regarding their salvation. Their eternal spirit is too valuable to God for us to be casual about where they will spend eternity. The Church must get a revelation of the heart of God toward the sinner. Have we forgotten where we, ourselves, came from?

Jesus told a parable about an unmerciful servant who owed a huge debt to the king. The king planned to imprison the servant's entire family, but the servant fell on his face and begged for patience, saying he would repay. The king had compassion and not only let him go free, but he cancelled his entire debt as well. Later, that same forgiven man found a fellow servant who owed him a relatively small amount of money and threw him in prison, ignoring his pleas for patience. When the king heard of the first servant's unmerciful action, he asked him why he didn't show the same mercy to his fellow servant that he had been shown. The king then turned him over to the jailers for torture (Matthew 18:21-35). All of us have been forgiven a massive debt that we have no way of paying. It is impossible for us to pay for our sin. The blood of Jesus is the only payment that could satisfy this debt and He freely shed it for us. We must offer the same forgiveness to others that our Savior has given to us. Along with voicing the Word of God without compromise, we must exhibit compassion for those outside of the church walls.

On another occasion in Matthew 7, Jesus addressed the topic of judging others. He said that before we try to remove a speck of dust out of another person's eye, we need to discern and remove the large plank that exists in our own eye. Can you imagine approaching a person to remove a splinter from their eye while you have a huge two-by-four jutting from your own eye? The person would be injured as a result of your board repeatedly striking them. The outcome will be the same if we approach a sinner without the proper heart motivation. Many people struggling with sin are hurt and dissuaded from following Jesus because of the attitude and the spirit with which Christians relate to them. A mature believer will approach a person in sin, remembering that they, themselves, were sinners who were forgiven by the grace and love of God as He dealt with them in truth and compassion. Following the example of God is the way the Church will most effectively reach the sinner.

So, Church, we must love. It is the only force that can break down walls and mend broken hearts. Jesus said in John 13:35, "Your love for one another will prove to the world that you are my disciples" (NLT). To many in the world, the Church does not represent love. We need to open our arms to those who are hurting. Many in the homosexual lifestyle have deep hurts in their lives. We can minister to those hurts.

Offering support and encouragement to families who are praying for a loved one who is in the lifestyle would be the Christlike action to take. Many families are suffering behind closed doors because no one talks about the topic of homosexuality. Parents are left thinking they are failures and not worthy to be used by God because of what their child is dealing with. Because of today's culture, there are very few people in our churches who have not been affected by a loved one who is in the lifestyle or is being subjected to those temptations.

The Church should open its doors to those who desire to leave the lifestyle. We have not taken the time to educate ourselves about homosexuality or how to minister to those who are struggling with the feelings. What would our response be to someone who walked into our church who was gay or lesbian? Would we gasp? Keep our distance? Judge? Or would we reach out in a way that shows genuine care? This can be done without condoning their sin.

Some may be led by God to allow a gay or lesbian who is looking for a way out, to live in their home for a period of time. This would not be easy and it would take a mature couple or individual for this to work, but this has proven to be successful. I know from personal experience. Many have never had a solid home life and are looking for a mentor. If we open our churches and homes to those struggling with homosexuality, think of the message it would send. Instead of "God hates fags," it would be "God loves you, and we love you too." Not everyone in the homosexual community is looking for a way out, but there are certainly many who are.

The Church need not forsake any fragment of truth as it relates to homosexuality, but must consider how it approaches the subject and how it ministers to those struggling. It must determine areas in which it has fallen short. The Church is called to hold up the banner of truth and the banner of love.

Chapter 17

How to Minister as the Church

Christians are called to be active participants in not only bringing people to Christ but in disciplining them according to biblical principles and Kingdom living. Here are some things to consider as you minister to someone struggling with homosexuality in your church or community.

Consult with experts working in this area. If you have not researched or done any studying in this area, you are already behind when a member or loved one struggling with same-sex attraction comes to you for help. By reading and speaking with people who have overcome this struggle, you can prepare yourself, your leaders, and your congregation to assist in the healing process. As Scripture tells us, "Refuse good advice and watch your plans fail; take good counsel and watch them succeed (Proverbs 15:22, MSG).

Assess the situation. Those who have struggled share many common experiences—abuse, rejection, and abandonment—however, every person is unique and not everything affects everyone the same way. Take the time to listen to people's stories so that you can get a better understanding of what they have been through and their issues. Assessing where they are will help you develop the road map to their healing.

Love them where they are. People who have struggled with same-sex attraction will have had detachment from their true masculine or feminine selves in varying degrees. Their outward appearance and speech may not match what you are accustomed to from a man or woman. They have often spent years developing what you see and hear on the outside, so you cannot expect it to all change overnight. You have to exemplify God's unconditional love, no matter what you see.

Lead them to where they are going. Once people make a decision to leave behind the homosexual lifestyle, they will begin a long, painful, and lonely journey. Perhaps their motive for seeking help comes simply from a desire to leave the lifestyle or maybe it is from having an encounter with Christ. Regardless, they will be looking to you for guidance. Here are three points to remember as you are helping someone go through the process of change.

1. The choice must be theirs and theirs alone. They have to make the decision to engage in the process, because they will have to do all of the work.

2. This process is done imperfectly, but it ultimately requires completely leaving the old behind. You can't have one foot in and the other one out. There is no "step down" process for coming out of this struggle—they

must go cold turkey. But make sure they do not feel pressured to do so. This must happen only when they are ready and not a moment sooner.

3. Surround them with support. When they have severed ties with those connected to this lifestyle, they will be left with a tremendous void. The following are different types of helpful support:

   - An Uplink—Identify someone who has already walked through this process who will be able to talk with and encourage them.
   - Accountability Partners—These will be people who are familiar with the process and the person's struggle with same-sex attraction. They must be committed to consistency in order to be a reliable force in their life.

No matter where someone fits in this process, accountability is crucial for all involved. As a spiritual leader, it is your responsibility to monitor the relationships of all those involved in order to ensure proper boundaries are kept and the one who is struggling does not end up in an inappropriate relationship with someone who is supposed to be helping them.

   - Restoration Team—These are individuals who may have never struggled with same-sex attractions, but are committed to other areas of this person's development. The focus of the team is to help restore to wholeness the spirit and soul of the person.

Janet Boynes Ministries is committed to helping keep families together, in spite of the situation going on in the home. We have trained spiritual leaders who are ready to help those who are struggling with same-sex attraction, as well as equip pastors and parents as they surround and minister to those who want out of the homosexual lifestyle. I would encourage you to call the ministry hotline listed at the end of the book.

As a person begins the process of deliverance, more issues may surface. The more they become comfortable with you, the more they may reveal. The road may be bumpy and they may even fall off track, but you must be committed for the long haul. You may find them going through times of anger, depression, and rebellion; do not take it personally. They are processing a lot and may be prone to lash out at those closest to them—which may be you.

It is tempting to want to fix the person. However, your ultimate goal is not to see someone walk out of homosexuality into heterosexuality but into wholeness and a path of obedience to Christ. If you sense that the person requires more help than you can provide, do not hesitate to refer them to professional counselors, physicians, or a valid ministry in order to address their underling emotional wounds and physical problems, which may have manifested due to their struggles. Do what you can do, and believe God will handle the rest.

A major key to success for people who are leaving any sinful habit or carnal desire is to teach them who they are in Christ. If they have given themselves to Christ by asking Jesus into their heart, then they have become a new creature in Christ, the old person has passed away and now all things are new (1 Corinthians 5:17). This may seem strange to the individual at first because from all outward appearances, they seem like the same person. They need to understand that it is their spirit that has become new. Their spirit is the real person and not their body, emotions, and mind.

Even someone who has been a Christian for many years may still be living by what they feel and think instead of by who God said they are in His Word. This is a defeated way to live and the joy of the Christian life will escape them. For example, someone struggling might say that they seem power-less when tempted with sin. But that is not what the Bible says about them. First John 5:4 says, "For every child of God defeats this evil world, and we achieve this victory through our faith"(NLT).

It is so important for the one who is struggling to begin seeing himself the way God sees him. God has placed every-thing needed inside his born-again spirit. The task is now to learn about all the spiritual weapons and all the attributes of the divine nature he now has access to. This is a process that all believers must go through if they desire to live a victorious, fruitful life. This is such an important truth.

People cry out to God asking Him to please deliver them, but Jesus already came and defeated sin. Now as His children, we must apply His victory to our own lives by renewing our minds with the spiritual truths found in the Bible. This will take perseverance. Our life experiences will begin to line up with who God says we are when we fill ourselves with His promises and speak them out of our own mouth. There is no sin that can dominate our lives when we walk in His Word and Spirit!

I want to share a story of a friend who reaches out and ministers to the gay community in an unconventional way.

My Experience as a Missionary to the Gay Community

What does it mean to love someone? I mean, what does it really look like to love a person? Now that's the million-dollar question; in fact, it may be the very reason you are reading this book. We look at this question, not only in the context of our immediate life, but also to understand our world's view. The current worldview is total acceptance of and empowerment to the gay community. In the context of our world's view and your own, I ask again: What does it mean to love someone?

Hello, my name is Jason. I am 27 years old and married to a lovely woman. I am a normal guy; I like sports, art, movies, and the outdoors. Maybe in some ways I'm not so normal, I am a conservative Christian. I believe in the Bible and what it says about homosexuality. Not a popular view, but the right view. Here is the kicker. With this view of God's standard of men and women, marriage and heterosexual relationships,

I am also a missionary to the gay community through gay pride festivals. Still with me? I would like to share what I have learned about love—the kind of love Jesus has for us—love without compromise, but with a desire to see people set free through the pure and simple message of the gospel.

First, let me share that I go with my parents to gay pride events, working alongside of them. They are my inspiration to do this. They have been doing it for years, faithful to the call God has placed on their lives. It is not an easy missionary field—who wants to go to a community that celebrates the gay lifestyle?

Over the years, people have asked my parents why they "cast their pearls before swine" (Matthew 7:6). To the average Christian, sex is a topic that is seldom discussed openly. To go to a place where sex is not only celebrated, but celebrated outside of God's original plan, seems downright foolish. So why do it? Why go to such great lengths to meet the gay community where they are at—a gay pride event? Love. Pure and simple.

My parents taught me that God has compassion for the person caught in the homosexual lifestyle. God showed my parents this is not a political issue of gay rights; it is about God wanting to set the homosexual male or the lesbian woman free. It is the message of the gospel—freedom. It is what He died for on the cross. Love.

It is important to see the person, not just the issue. I have had the privilege of participating in this missionary field and sharing the good news of Christ. My parents and I have hearts of compassion and desire to give out the message of Christ by handing out free Bibles, sharing our testimony, listening to their stories, and just loving on them. Galatians 5:14 says, "For the whole law can be summed up in this one command: 'Love your neighbor as yourself'" (NLT). The gay community is not our enemy, and Christians should not be theirs. We have seen God do amazing things through this mission field as we are compelled to reach a group of people who are not certain of our motives or our love.

So back to our original question: What does it mean to love somebody? It is caring enough for them to share the gospel. It is caring enough to want to see them set free. It is caring enough to love, even when they are unlovable. It is following God's example and leading. God cared enough to send His Son to die on the cross, that none should perish. That is the truest love of all.

—JJ

Chapter 18

PRAYER

In the days ahead, you are going to have to find your own war room. Yes, I said war room. A room where you do battle. A room where you stand in prayer for those you love. Perhaps that room has a Bible, a pencil, paper, a chair, and a light. It is a room where you meet with God and do battle against the spirit of darkness.

People are used to doing battle with their hands and their mouths, but they don't know how to fight in the spirit, where the supernatural will give birth to the natural. Luke 22:31-32 says, "Simon, stay on your toes. Satan has tried his best to separate all of you from me, like chaff from wheat. Simon, I've prayed for you in particular that you not give in or give out. When you have come through the time of testing, turn to your companions and give them a fresh start" (MSG).

The Lord called him Simon instead of Peter because He knew that Peter would act out of his old nature (Simon). God is aware of our human weakness. Jesus knew beforehand that Peter would deny Him. Yet when his time of testing was over and after he had repented, he was asked to give his companions a fresh start. The lost need you and I to battle for them in prayer. Sometimes we have to go to that little war room and cry out to the Lord for our loved ones. I personally know several Christians who have turned away from following Jesus. Perhaps it was a tragedy that caused them to walk away from a loving God or simply the desire to do their own will. Regardless, we need to keep praying so their eyes will be opened.

"Jesus said to them, 'If God were your father, you would love Me. I came from God. I did not come on My own, but God sent Me. Why do you not understand what I say? It is because you do not want to hear My teaching. The devil is your father. You are from him. You want to do the sinful things your father, the devil, wants you to do. He has been a killer from the beginning. The devil has nothing to do with the truth. There is no truth in him. It is expected of the devil to lie, for he is a liar and the father of lies. I tell you the truth and that is why you do not put your trust in Me. Which one of you can say I am guilty of sin? If I tell you the truth, why do you not believe Me? Whoever is born of God listens to God's Word. You do not hear His Word because you are not born of God'" (John 8:42-47 NLV). Those who are not serving God, are under the power and authority of Satan. Acts 26:18 says that the enemy has blinded the spiritual eyes of those who are not serving God. Listen, saints. The enemy has no greater desire than to blind the minds of the lost, specifically to keep them from understanding the gospel.

When I backslid for 14 years, I had no desire to serve God. I was too caught up in my own sin. I no longer wanted to hear the voice of the Lord, nor did I care what He had to say.

The enemy knew how to keep me busy by putting women and drugs in front of me so I would not think of the things of God. I was distracted by my own sin. So what I ended up doing was rejecting the person who would help me the most, and that was Jesus Christ.

Jesus is here in our lives wanting to open our ears, wanting to guide the message in our hearts, but our hearts aren't open to receive His everlasting love. The light has always been shining in our lives, but we have no desire to receive it. Unless the Holy Spirit removes the blinders and opens our mind and heart to the gospel, we will never have a desire to receive it. There will be many who will not be saved, not because God doesn't desire that for them, but because the things of God are foolishness to them (1 Corinthians 2:14).

The Greek word for foolishness is *moria*, from which we get our word *moron*, which means stupid or mentally retarded. The lost person sees the gospel as moronic and stupid.

We must learn to pray effectively for those who are lost. I think our greatest example in the Bible is Jesus. Isaiah 53 says that Christ made intercession for the transgressors. "My prayer is not for the world, but for those you have given me, because they belong to you" (John 17:9, NLT).

The same way Jesus prays for us, we need to plead and learn how to pray effectively for those we love. It may be our prayers that change the direction of their lives. Just as Jesus did, we must pray according to the Word of God. Jesus only did what He saw the Father do (John 5:19). Jesus is forever making intercession for us; He is our negotiator. None of us are relieved from our post or responsibility of interceding for our loved ones or others. As it says in Isaiah 41:21, we should present our case to the Lord. When you have loved ones who are backslidden or have never accepted Christ as Lord and Savior, you should want to travail in prayer for them.

That brings me to the story of Hannah and Peninnah. Hannah's story is so fascinating to me because she believed for something that she could not see with the naked eye, but in the spirit she knew God would bring it to pass. Hannah wanted a child—a son—but it wasn't happening. Peninnah taunted Hannah because she was barren. How many times have you prayed knowing you heard from God, but it was not coming to pass in your time frame? God promised Hannah a son, but it wasn't looking very good. When Hannah got tired of feeling sorry for herself, she went to God in prayer.

The Bible says "Hannah was in deep anguish, crying bitterly as she prayed to the LORD" (1 Samuel 1:10, NLT). Hannah was discouraged and just poured her heart out to the Lord. When are we going to get on our face and cry out to the Lord for our family, friend or loved one? When Hannah did travail before the Lord, things happened. The Bible says she slept with her husband Elkanah and God remembered her plea. Hannah had a son. Read the story in the first chapter of Samuel 1.

We won't fully know the impact our prayers have for people until we stand before the Lord. We can't give up just because we can't see the Lord's hand working; let's keep in mind He never sleeps or slumbers. Let me say this, family of God, love should be our biggest motivation for praying for the lost and our loved ones. In the words of Billy Graham, "It is the Holy Spirit's job to convict, God's job to judge, and our job to love." We must have faith in order to win those who are lost.

Do you know that the entire universe was formed at God's command, that what we now see did not come from anything that can be seen? When God created the earth, it was all by spoken word. It wasn't what He saw that created the world. It was by what He said. It is the same thing with our families; we have to stretch our faith to believe what we can't see, in order for our families to return to the Lord. It will be our faith and our spoken words that will bring our families back to the Lord.

Our spoken words are good, but it also doesn't hurt to put in corresponding action. Remember the story in Mark 2, of the paralytic who was carried by four men to see Jesus? Go back and read the story. These men found a way to get what they needed, no matter who or what stood in the way. When they realized the room where Jesus was teaching was too crowded and there was no entry to get to Jesus, look at what these geniuses did. "They couldn't bring him to Jesus because of the crowd, so they dug a hole through the roof above his head. Then they lowered the man on his mat, right down in front of Jesus" (Mark 2:4, NLT).

Faith is the ticket to the Kingdom, or should I say to heaven. God will supply all of our needs when needed. To all the families that doubt God when it comes to their child, God doesn't have a problem with healing your family member, friend or setting them free from homosexuality.

Even after loved ones believe God for their salvation, some choose not to leave the life of homosexuality. This is not because their loved ones had a lack of faith or were ineffective in prayer, it's because they are free moral agents. They have a will, and God will not force anyone to do anything against their free will.

God wants us to love Him because we want to, not because we have to. The Bible says, "If a man has a hundred sheep and one of them gets lost, what will he do? Won't he leave the ninety-nine others in the wilderness and go to search for the one that is lost until he finds it?" (Luke 15:4, NLT) The Lord will continue to do His part, but ultimately we have to yield to His calling. "Look! I stand at the door and knock. If you hear my voice and open the door, I will come in, and we will share a meal together as friends" (Revelation 3:20, NLT).

The Bible credits mighty power to prayer. The Bible says prayer is powerful. "Therefore, confess your sins to one another and pray for one another, that you may be healed. The prayer of a righteous person has great power as it is working" (James 5:16, ESV).

In Greek, the word *fervent* means" to be active and efficient." When Christians pray in faith, we have the capacity to activate God's power in order to reach those we love. Think about Elijah when he prayed to God in 1 Kings 18:36-37: "At the usual time for offering the evening sacrifice, Elijah the prophet walked up to the altar and prayed, 'O LORD, God of Abraham, Isaac, and Jacob, prove today that you are God in Israel and that I am your servant. Prove that I have done all this at your command. O LORD, answer me! Answer me so these people will know that you, O LORD, are God and that you have brought them back to yourself'" (NLT). He was praying under the order of God. Elijah was asking God to answer him and reveal to the people that He was who He said He was and that He was giving the people another chance to repent.

After Elijah prayed, immediately, the fire of God fell and burned up the offering, the wood, the stone, the dirt, and even the water in the trench. All the people saw it happen and fell on their faces in awe and worship, exclaiming, "God is the true God" (1 Kings 38-39).

My question to you is, do you live by faith or by sight? Do you have to see something before you believe God is capable? Consider Jesus' words to Thomas, "You believe because you have seen me. Blessed are those who believe without seeing me" (John 20:29, NLT).

God really wants us to witness the power of prayer. If we don't have a biblical basis for praying for the lost or family other than the fact that God expects us to, this would be enough for me. What the Lord has shown me over the years is that persistence in prayer is a necessary factor.

The Bible says in Isaiah 14:17 that the lost are prisoners of Satan. If the devil doesn't release our loved ones, we have to find a way to tie the devil up. "Who is powerful enough to enter the house of a strong man like Satan and plunder his goods? Only someone even stronger—someone who could tie him up and then plunder his house" (Mark 3:27, NLT). We have to understand that some demons are so strong, we have to pray and fast in order to gain the victory. Just know that the devil does not want to let our loved ones go. We are going to have to pray and fast, as it says in Mark 9:29.

The enemy wants to make our situations look so impossible that we get discouraged and quit praying. There is nothing our God can't do. If we quit praying, we fall into the enemy's trap. The devil has no defense against our prayers. Our prayers are so powerful that when we do pray, the devil tries to distract us by allowing the phone to ring, having us think about washing clothes, or planning dinner. Keep praying because when you pray, Satan loses his mind.

We have to remember that our prayers are a form of warfare. When we pray, Satan is being defeated even when we don't see any changes in the natural. Our circumstances may change, but our faith should never change.

There was a time when I had to believe God in order to go into full-time ministry. I knew He had called me but I wasn't released from my full-time job yet. I prayed for the peace of God to release me. Four years later, I heard the words in my spirit, "You are released." Since then, faith and prayer have become a major part of my everyday life.

Sometimes, we just have to plead to God for our loved ones. Abraham pleaded for Sodom (Genesis 18). Moses pleaded for Israel (Exodus 32). Hezekiah pleaded for Judah (2 Kings 19).

When we plead to God, we are asking Him to intervene. We can plead the purposes of God (Jeremiah 1:5). We can plead the promises of God concerning salvation (John 3:16). We can plead the power of God to save (Hebrews 7:25). Jesus said, "If you abide in Me, and My words abide in you, you will ask what you desire and it shall be done for you (John 15:7, NKJV).

| Chapter 19 |

DEAR PASTOR

I'm grieved because I stood on the edge of losing my faith; not my faith in God, but my faith in people. I wonder how long those who struggle will cry out to their pastors and churches only to be told once again, "We don't deal with the issue of homosexuality." I have personally heard some pastors say, "We can talk about it next year." I think this is their way of avoiding the issue.

From speaking at many churches, I have learned that we, as the body of Christ, are not of the same mind on how to address the topic of homosexuality, same-sex attraction, and transgender issues. Maybe you are a pastor who is on the fence when it comes to talking about LGBT issues. Or perhaps you just don't know what to believe anymore or even how to deal with this in your church. If that's you, this chapter is for you. Homosexuality is the elephant in the room that we can no longer ignore. It is dividing churches, families, marriages, and political parties across America.

We are at a place where if we preach about materialism, we might offend rich people in the audience. We can't preach about fornication because there are people in the church who are living together. We can't preach about domestic violence because there is a deacon or pastor who might be abusing his wife. And we can't preach against homosexuality because our culture says that's hateful.

The Bible is clear on the issue of homosexuality the same way it is clear when referring to a lying tongue, proud heart, and many other things mentioned in Proverbs 6:16-19. I am hoping that pastors will come alongside those of us who have experience and credibility on this issue so we may help you assist those who want to leave the lifestyle.

As we continue our effort to help those struggling in their efforts to be free from homosexuality, I am finding that we have neglected the first step—clarifying our own scriptural understanding of homosexuality. We are gripped with fear of the backlash that can come from addressing it in our congregations. I know this, because I experience it on a regular basis.

We have far too many broken and hopeless individuals who are merely walking in the shadows of who they were created to be. Pastors, what we are dealing with today isn't just a sexuality crisis, it's an identity crisis. So many are clueless about who they are and who God created them to be. The church ought to be a place of gathering that is equipped to help free those who are struggling with homosexuality, transgenderism, and even homophobia. The Bible says in Matthew 9:11-13, "Later when Jesus was eating supper at Matthew's house with his close followers, a lot of disreputable characters came and joined them. When the Pharisees saw him keeping this kind of company, they had a fit, and lit into Jesus' followers. 'What kind of example is this from your Teacher, acting cozy with crooks and riffraff?' Jesus, overhearing, shot back, 'Who needs a doctor, the healthy or the sick? Go figure out what this Scripture means: "I'm after mercy, not religion." I'm here to invite outsiders, not coddle insiders'" (MSG).

When the Word of God comes forth, it is powerful; it cuts between the soul and the spirit. "For the word of God is alive and powerful. It is sharper than the sharpest two-edged sword, cutting between soul and spirit, between joint and marrow. It exposes our innermost thoughts and desires" (Hebrew 4:12, NLT). If freedom is going to come to anyone, it will come from the Word of God that is preached in our services. What am I asking of you? I am asking you, as a pastor, to do what you do so eloquently every Sunday, preach the Word of God. It isn't about preaching guilt or condemnation. The gospel is about the truth that sets us free. We are sinners saved by grace. Grace empowers us to overcome sin.

People dealing with same-sex attraction are no different than any other person in your congregation. Let's keep in mind that, as Paul said, we all fall short of God's glory. Yet what I know from living the lifestyle is the agony a homosexual can face when entering a church. What I believed (and what I know many still believe) is that unless we become heterosexuals, we will not be accepted into the body of Christ.

No one is perfect but Jesus. We have to stop trying to be "God junior." We all struggle with some sort of sin that we personally wish would just go away. Some sins are more obvious than others. If we as the Church could give those struggling with homosexuality spiritual and sexual guidance, we would be doing a great service to them as they struggle to leave the homosexual lifestyle.

We have a standard to uphold, and God's standard is non-negotiable. There are many from the gay community who desperately go to God for help, praying without ceasing, begging for the thoughts and desires to go away. Salvation does not mean that we never again have sinful thoughts, desires, or temptations. We will all experience these things until Christ returns. However, as we grow in Christ, we learn to walk as overcomers.

As pastors, ministry leaders, deacons, or leaders in the church, we must minister to all, including those who are struggling with homosexuality. Let us not categorize sins as one being bigger than the other. We are all in need of God's grace. Pastors, you are the agents of reconciliation in your church.

We should minister with gentleness and grace. Solomon wrote in Ecclesiastes 4:9-10, "Two are better than one, for they can help each other succeed. If one person falls, the other can reach out and help" (NLT). We all stumble and fall in our own way. But let's not think that a particular sin or temptation is more outrageous than another, mainly because it is not what we experience. Every temptation we face, at its core, was faced by Jesus, yet He was without sin. The temptation to give in to same-sex desire is no more terrible than an enticement to heterosexual lust. We can either force each other to struggle alone against such temptations or we can be the body of Christ and lift each other up in the heat of the struggle and war. My desire is to help with gentleness and grace, remembering the struggle and agony I face in my own temptations.

Remember when ministering to those struggling, that sexual-identity is a choice, same-sex attraction is not. We can't help who we are attracted to. To the gay community, their emotions and sexual desires are as real and strong to them as those between people in a heterosexual relationship. God most definitely wants us to have our sexuality in order, and He can help us in the process of change.

So many times, we want to change people from gay to straight. We must not focus only on their sexuality. Let's be more concerned about their spirituality. What I find is that if we disciple and encourage individuals to have a relationship with Jesus, they will find freedom from homosexuality, just as I have.

As I travel and speak on the issue of homosexuality, many people ask me how they can get help at their local church. I reply, "Talk with your pastor." The response is shocking. They hear things like, "We don't deal with that here," or "You need to go to another church." Sometimes they are told that someone will get back to them, and they never hear back. Those who suffer in silence often have a fear of talking with their pastor or ministry leader. Whether they are right or wrong, they believe that going to their pastors would be of no help to them. What is their fear? They fear that they will be humiliated in front of the church and rejected.

Pastors, let me give you a few suggestions on what you can talk about from the pulpit that will allow those who struggle to get help and know that you are on their side. Be sure to come across as someone they can talk to who will offer encouragement and even a safe place for them. Let them know they will not have to walk this journey alone. Direct them to be involved in a small group and provide resource materials that will let them know they don't have to stay in the same place.

I would also suggest that you establish church doctrine regarding your position on homosexuality, same-sex attraction, and transgenderism. Now is the time to be proactive and prepare for what may happen in the future regarding same-sex marriage relationships. What is your stand regarding same-sex marriage? Thinking about these issues now and being prepared may help deter problems later on for you and your church.

"There's nothing like the written Word of God for showing you the way to salvation through faith in Christ Jesus. Every part of Scripture is God-breathed and useful one way or another—showing us truth, exposing our rebellion, correcting our mistakes, training us to live God's way. Through the Word we are put together and shaped up for the tasks God has for us" (2 Timothy 3:16-17, MSG). Pastors, broken people will find freedom in your churches when the Word of God is preached. You, as the shepherd, are equipped to empower the body of Christ. Rely heavily on the resurrection power of God. We are merely His agents. It is the Holy Spirit who carries out the transforming work in every person. I believe in compassion without compromise.

REAL LIFE,
REAL STORIES

Chapter 20

THE HEART OF A PARENT

Our Story

We are thankful for the opportunity to share our story, and we believe it will be an encouragement to others. We have been married for over 33 years, and we have been involved in ministry through our church in one way or another since we first began dating. God grew our family through the realm of adoption and we were miraculously blessed with two beautiful baby girls.

When our oldest daughter came to us at around age 14 and shared that she thought she might be a lesbian, our world was rocked and we were devastated. She had scriptures lined up as to why homosexuality was wrong and assured us that she had a handle on the issue. We let her know that we supported and loved her and that we felt she would walk away from this. We believe that there was a seed planted at a young age (seventh grade) when a friend at school approached her and asked her if she was a lesbian. Her response at the time was, "What is a lesbian?" As someone who loved sports very much and felt (in her words), a little "awkward most of the time around people," this thought stayed around in her head and took root as she got older.

As we watched our daughter battle with same-sex attraction as she grew older, we walked through many feelings and emotions. We had feelings of failure, incompleteness, and even shame. We had a desire to help our daughter through it all, but did not really know exactly what to do or where to turn. It is painful to watch your child go through struggles. We have walked through these feelings and many others by the grace of God, knowing that we can do all things through Christ who strengthens us. We have made the decision to trust God during times such as these and to never stop believing that His hand is strong enough to work in both us and in our children to accomplish His goals for our lives. We have been given supernatural peace and determination over the years to stand on God's promises, and now, we reach out to other parents who may be experiencing what we experienced.

We have always made it clear to our daughter that we love her unconditionally; she is always welcome at home (she lives out of state). At the same time, we expressed that we cannot condone the lifestyle or her involvement in any unhealthy relationship. We have set boundaries and do not allow a partner to stay in our home overnight or be a part of family holiday activities. We have let our daughter know that even though we cannot affirm a same-sex relationship, we affirm her as a person and will never stop loving her, despite the decisions she makes. She also knows that we pray daily that she will walk in the plan God has for her life.

We have learned many things throughout this challenging time. It is unfortunate that when we first learned of our daughter's feelings, there was so little help for parents and for those struggling. It seemed this was a subject that was either ignored or treated with condemnation. We've learned that there is usually a root cause for someone dealing with homosexuality, and the lifestyle is just a symptom of a deeper need or hurt.

Another lesson we learned is that we must move forward with our lives and not become emotionally and spiritually "frozen" in time. We must allow God, through the Holy Spirit, to continually change us into who He created us to be. Our lives should be lights that will draw those who are lost and struggling. Our home should reflect Romans 14:17 which says, "The Kingdom of God is…righteousness, peace and joy in the Holy Spirit" (NIV). Our loved one will not be drawn to us and to the Lord if we are always depressed and stressed out!

At this time, we have a vision for our daughter that we hold on to and choose to focus on instead of the circumstances that we see with our eyes. We have a vision to see her walking in freedom with a close relationship with the Father; we see her walking in peace instead of turmoil. We have shared with her that God's standards for marriage and the family do not change, and that is the reason why we cannot approve of the relationship she may be in, even if society accepts and promotes same-sex unions and relationships.

We wanted to share our story in hope that it would speak to other families with similar backgrounds and stories. The biggest lesson we have learned through our experiences is to trust God when the problems are bigger than we can handle ourselves and to never give up on our children, as He has never given up on us. We also have determined to continue serving in ministry and giving to others even while we are waiting to see the promises fulfilled in our own lives.

—T & J

A Mother's Broken Heart

I suppose I found out about my daughter the way many parents do—after she had been living the lifestyle for a few years. If I am honest with myself, I knew the signs were there long before I "officially" found out.

Hi, my name is Melanie, and I have a 21-year-old daughter who has been living as a lesbian since she was 13. I often ask myself if things could be different right now, if there was something I could have changed, and at times the thought drives me crazy.

I had tried for many years to get pregnant. My husband and I had a couple miscarriages, infertility testing, scheduled intercourse, and finally infertility medications to try and conceive a child. After seven years, it happened. The pregnancy test was positive. I remember being ecstatic and terrified at the same time. I did not want to lose this pregnancy. At 12 weeks, I had an ultrasound that confirmed a heartbeat. Our prayers were answered. She was a happy baby, and everything about her was perfect to me. She wore dresses, laughed all the time, and I loved her like crazy.

She began dressing more in boy T-shirts and basketball shorts in seventh and eighth grade. She liked boys' shoes and short hair. I just thought it was a phase. She was heavier and said she felt more comfortable in those clothes. She had a hard time making friends, was very emotional and immature in her relationships. She is a smart girl, but did not apply herself. When she was struggling, her dad and I missed many opportunities to help her navigate the issues. I believe it is true what Janet says, that often there is trauma in children's lives that lead them to seek alternatives to fill the pain. I won't go into the details, but my daughter experienced many things she shouldn't have. Her dad and I had many of our own issues that affected our parenting ability. She was not as nurtured or valued as she should have been, and thus began questioning her worth. For a while, she found her worth in the church. Eventually, she found it as a ninth grader in a new school, when another girl came up to her and told her she was beautiful. One night she was staying over at her new best friend's home, and the girl kissed her. And so it began.

I started wondering what was going on between her and her best friend when I found notes in her room that seemed too intimate for best friends. But I did not push the issue. I should have. When her best friend broke up with her at the start of their senior year, I found out the truth. They had been dating, had been intimate, and I was devastated.

God has brought me through my guilt regarding my daughter. I have apologized to her for not being there for her and for not protecting her. I have grown and matured as I have listened to how God wants me to be in relationship with my daughter. She is a beautiful, young woman, and so much more than her sexual identity. She is musically gifted, giving, forgiving, caring, funny, hard-working, and intelligent. She shares her life with me, and although she knows I do not support this lifestyle choice, she knows I support her, love her unconditionally, and pray for her.

Isaiah 54:13 says, "I will teach all your children, and they will enjoy great peace" (NLT). That is His promise to me. I believe it and stand on His promise daily.

–M.E.

Our Family's Experience With a Son Who Has Given in to Same-sex Attraction

My wife and I have three children—two daughters and, in the middle, a son. They all grew up intimately involved in the conservative, Bible-believing church we attended. Our son, Ethan, was especially active in the youth group, went on mission trips, and followed the Lord. In fact, his best friend was the pastor's son. As is the case with many who struggle with same-sex attractions, Ethan was very gifted in the creative arts like music and acting.

When he was 19 and a music intern at our church, Ethan abruptly changed the entire direction of his life. Over a period of just a few weeks, he moved from being a seemingly content Christian to a rebel who started smoking, drinking, experimenting with drugs, and thinking that he might be gay. We do not yet know what exactly happened to him at that time. We only know that soon after that, he left our family, moved away, and immersed himself in the gay lifestyle.

Our family was miffed. How could he choose that? We were confused, disappointed, angry, embarrassed, and at a complete loss for what to do. We started looking for people who had been through this, for counselors, and for resources. There wasn't much available. We poured out our hearts to the Lord (Psalm 62:8), ceased striving, and trusted God (Psalm 46:10), and embraced 2 Chronicles 20:12 which says, "We do not know what to do, but we are looking to you for help" (NLT). After two years of trying everything suggested to us to get our son back, we symbolically placed him in a basket of reeds and shoved him out into crocodile-infested waters...just like Moses' mother did with her son.

Ethan was barely in touch with us over the next ten years or so, moving from city to city, partner to partner, and drug to drug. Sometimes he would contact us when he was flat broke. When he was about 30, we found him, again expressed to him our love for him, and challenged him to change the direction of his life. I remember him saying, "Dad, I haven't got any money, a place to live, food, a job, a cellphone, or anything on my schedule for at least five years." It was heart-breaking. However, God used that day as a turning point in his life. He expressed a desire to get serious about starting a career and getting off drugs. We helped him get a car, a place to live, and a job.

Over time, he became a wonderful, much-loved part of our family again. His sisters, their spouses, and our grandchildren all loved having Uncle Ethan back. He came to all of our family events again, often bringing people with him. For a young man who failed out of three colleges, his career started slowly but has blossomed into more than we imagined it would. He has progressed from scanning 36,000 documents per day to helping set direction for a significant international company.

Don't imagine that our relationship has been a smooth one. Ethan knows that we have "compassion without compromise" when it comes to how we feel about homosexuality. In other words, we have compassion for each individual who struggles with same-sex attraction, but we firmly stand against every part of the radical homosexual movement. In contrast with his view growing up, he now believes that he was "born that way" and that we are still too narrow in our thinking.

We have probably met over 200 of his gay friends at our home. While they are welcome to come over for casual food and conversation, they are no longer welcome at family events following a really unfortunate Thanksgiving experience with one of them. Ethan and my relationship does not fit the typical father-son model that most gay men experience. In other words, he and I have a good relationship, not an absent or combative one. In fact, one night, Ethan asked me to join him and about a dozen of his gay friends, none of whom had any kind of positive relationship with their fathers. It was a tearful time hearing the stories of the pain that those young men without father-son relationships had experienced.

About once a year, Ethan and I have a "no holds barred" conversation that is very direct and usually loud at times. I challenge his thinking and decisions, and he again expresses his frustration that I don't see things his way. We talk again about same-sex attraction versus homosexual acts. After about an hour of that, we grin, hug, express our love for one another, and know that we will have this discussion again in the future.

Currently, Ethan is planning to marry a gay man with whom he is living. He has now had individual conversations with all members of our family in an effort to solicit support for his decision and perhaps attendance at the ceremony. All of the family members have responded with professions of love for him, but he has consistently been told they will not support something that is clearly condemned by God in Scripture. His family will not recognize him as a married person if he goes through a civil ceremony, and his partner will never be welcomed in our home as a member of our family. We realize that might sound harsh to some, but our reasons for that position are pretty sound. First, we see what Ethan's participation in that lifestyle has cost him and us. Second, we understand the extreme health risks and shortened life expectancy associated with homosexuality. Finally, we see only condemnation for homosexual acts in the Bible. We believe that families have to ask themselves, "Can we help our son or daughter more by condoning their lifestyle or by telling them the truth?" Which would you tell an alcoholic?

I have had the opportunity to share our experience with junior high and high school students, college students, churches, and many families. It is painful beyond words to watch your child exchange your family's faith and values for the counterfeit values of homosexuality.

Billy Graham was asked one time what he would do if he had a gay son. He said, "I guess that we would have to love him more." We agree, and we'll keep trusting our Ethan to God.

—G.L.

My Journey

In March 2007, we had just finished funeral services for my mom. My heart was broken over losing her. Our daughter, who was 24 at the time, came for the service. She lived three hours away.

For several months prior, I had been planning a surprise birthday party for my husband's 60th birthday. The date previously set for the party ended up falling on the weekend after my mom's funeral. Our daughter came to help decorate and visit with all the people at the party. We had a wonderful time. My husband, daughter, and I had a wonderful relationship. We spent a lot of time together when she lived with us, and we were always very close.

A week after the events, I received an email at work from our daughter stating she was a lesbian, was in a relationship, and she was "born that way." She also emailed me links to several websites to look at that talked about homosexuality so I would be excited about her new announcement. I cried. I was a wreck. I called my close friend and co-worker to come to my office to read the email. She was very supportive and stood by my side.

My husband and I were devastated. From that day until now as I write this, we have not had a relationship with our daughter. Since we do not agree with the lifestyle, she wants nothing to do with us. We do not hear from her at birthdays,

Mother's Day, Father's Day, or holidays. She came over once to the house years ago but the conversation was limited. We've talked only a few times (less than ten) over these past eight years. The times we have talked over the phone, the conversation has been very strained. The second time she stopped by the house years ago, she refused to come in, so I talked to her outside. She was disrespectful because we weren't excited about her decision and still would not agree with the lifestyle choice she made. This lifestyle is a choice. She was not born this way. God creates us all uniquely; He does not make mistakes. In her last email to me at work years ago, she said she didn't want to be contacted when we die. This was not the daughter we raised.

Our close friends pray for us, which helps a great deal. My husband and I also attended some godly counseling sessions with a local pastor. This helped us tremendously. The pastor explained that the core of who our daughter is and how she was raised is still there and will always be there. Some day she will come back to the core of who she is in Christ. We carried a lot of guilt and expressed many different emotions at the beginning. Later, I found Janet Boynes' Ministry on the Internet. I sent an email about our daughter and asked for help. To my surprise, Janet called me that same evening. She was sent to me by God. She listened to me, encouraged and prayed for me. Also, Janet introduced me to other moms whose kids are in the lifestyle.

Janet's ministry held weekly prayer line calls. This helped me tremendously. Through this ministry and prayer, I started growing in my relationship with God. I thought I had a strong relationship with God in the past, but now I realize I was a timid, baby Christian. Janet helped me deepen my faith and walk with the Lord. I will always be grateful to Janet for everything she has done for me.

Eight years later, I am confident in my faith. I still have a long way to go. I share God's Word with others. I lead a Bible study to share His message. I continue to visit with other moms whose kids are in the lifestyle. We understand how each other feels. We pray for our kids, and we pray for each other. Prayers make a difference. God is with us through this journey. I feel His presence.

My husband and I were honored to meet Janet in person in April 2015. She has helped me to be the person I am today as I serve the Lord. I will be forever grateful. I feel I have a ministry of encouraging others. God is good, and He has an amazing plan for our daughter and for us. It's our destiny to help and encourage others. We will be bold and courageous for Him. My husband and I pray every day thanking God in advance for bringing our daughter home. We love her very much; we miss her a lot and look forward to seeing her soon. Only God can restore our relationship.

Thank You, Jesus, for Your grace, mercy, and love. Thank You, Jesus, for carrying me through this journey. God is our Healer.

—J.M.

How Could My Daughter Be Gay? She's a Pastor's Kid.

When I discovered that my daughter was gay, I was devastated, to say the least. As I reflect back over the years leading up to my discovery, there were small indicators along the way. I did not consider these incidences as real reasons for concern because homosexuality was not on my radar. But one time there was a young woman in our church who complained to me that my daughter was continuously calling her on the phone. She saved the messages and allowed me to hear them. The messages consisted of my daughter telling her how beautiful she was and how much she liked her. She must have called this woman 20 times. When my daughter realized her calls were not cute, but a bother, she stopped calling this woman. There were other women, mostly older, who came to me sharing my daughter's inappropriate behavior that was occurring in different ways. It appeared as if my daughter was forming attachments to older women.

Then came "the letter." One day, I found a letter addressed to me from her, stating she was leaving home and moving to another state. I later found out she had been communicating with a young lady she had met online and was going to move closer so that she could develop a relationship with her. I then realized what I was dealing with: *My daughter is gay*. It felt as if a truck slammed into me, and I fell under the pressure and completely lost all consciousness.

My thoughts became wild, centering on my daughter 24/7. I felt shame, sadness, anger, fear, desperation and hopelessness all at the same time. How could my daughter be gay? She came from a Christian home and was raised in the church. We were church leaders. Her father was the senior pastor of the church. I couldn't figure out how this was all playing out. How could we shepherd a church and have a gay daughter? Why would God bring this crashing blow of a situation into our home?

In my lifetime, I have crawled out of a lot of bad places, but with this situation, I didn't even know which direction to turn. I didn't want this trouble and pain in my life. Personally, I felt I could have handled any other pressure besides this. I would have adjusted better finding out my daughter was pregnant than gay. At least being pregnant meant she was involved with a boy in a natural man and woman relationship. There was nothing natural about my daughter being gay. I sought answers. I read every book I could get my hands on dealing with this subject. I cried and prayed a lot. Many people in my church knew about my daughter. It appeared I was the last one on board to fully come to terms with her lifestyle. I simply had no room in my mind for such conduct.

I didn't know who I could talk to about my pain, so I went to see a Christian counselor. The sessions were good, but what has brought real healing (and healing even until today) has been prayer and learning to trust God with my daughter. I came to a place where I handed her over to God. All of her confusion, as well as my own, had to become the business of God Almighty. My daily challenge is to keep it in His hands where it belongs. Even though some individuals in my church knew about my daughter, I didn't want to share her situation with them because I didn't want people to judge her for her behavior. I also found out about a weekly conference call where parents with children who are homosexuals would pray together. Sometimes individuals caught in the lifestyle could call in, wanting deliverance; or sometimes, someone who had been delivered would get on the line. The prayers directed at the homosexual population encouraged my heart in amazing ways. I felt encouraged every time I hung up the phone that my daughter, too, would be delivered.

As I write this, my daughter is still involved in this lifestyle. I am trusting God each day to get me through. I hold on to the verse of Scripture that says, "For this reason I also suffer these things; nevertheless I am not ashamed, for I know whom I have believed and am persuaded that He is able to keep what I have committed to Him until that Day" (2 Timothy 1:12, NKJV).

—M.O.

Faithfulness of the Lord

Our challenges began 30 years ago when our son was 25. He'd always been a son we could be proud of, and he was so easy to love. However, the day he told us he was gay was the beginning of our journey in understanding the faithfulness of God.

Ever since our son entered the gay lifestyle, he has pushed for more acceptance of the homosexual identity he has chosen. We, as his parents, feel that the seed was planted after he experienced two rejections that came at the same time and his bitterness was very obvious. He had broken up with a very special girl in college and had gone to win her back. Yet it didn't work out as he planned. About that same time, he was denied entrance into an Ivy League school. Since he had always excelled in whatever he pursued, these things seemed to be more than he could or would accept.

Our son was a believer before he entered the lifestyle. But since joining this culture, he has denied his faith, becoming an unhappy and critical person. He has drifted in and out of our lives, and about 18 months ago, broke all relations with us. Until that time, we still had a relationship, despite his lifestyle choice. Our other son has been able to have lunch with his brother and has tried to help him understand how wrong his choice is according to the Word. He points out to his brother how much he has changed since making his choice. He can see that his prodigal brother is sad and feels hopeless but is also extremely determined that he is gay. We are sad that there is no relationship with him right now, but he knows we love him, and we know he still loves us….and God. We all will welcome him home anytime.

People ask how we do it. It has been 30 years. We read and memorize Scripture, pray and stay involved in church. We have grown in our faith and in our marriage, uniting in our desire to stand for the Lord. We walk in joy because the Lord has grown and matured us. We pray for our son and never give up hope that he will reject the sin and return to the Lord.

The Lord has been our close companion through this. We will continue to pray and love our son, but will never compromise the Word of God. Our hope is in the Lord, and we will walk in the faithfulness God has not only showed us, but also taught us.

—C.E.

Through My Eyes: Life with a Lesbian Mom

I was born in St. Paul, Minnesota, to my two very young parents who were dating when they had me. My mother is African American, Native American, and Mexican, and my dad is Caucasian, Native American, and Mexican. My mom and dad broke up when I was around one or two years old. From that time on, I was passed back and forth between them. Sometimes I would stay with my mom, and other times with my dad. I grew up thinking this was normal and didn't mind going back and forth. When I was with my dad, I could spend time with my grandma and grandpa, family, and cousins who were the same age as us. With my mom, I could be the only child. To me it was a win-win situation. However, in reality there were many negative aspects of my childhood.

Sometimes I would have to wait for hours for my mom to pick me up. She'd change her phone number so I'd have to track her down. Mom never had a consistent job, so keeping up with the phone bill was not a priority. With my dad, he wasn't always around, so I spent a lot of time with my grandparents.

At age 11, my mother came to see me. She had told me a few months earlier that she was pregnant. She had been sleeping with a friend and got pregnant. The "friend" decided he wasn't ready to be a dad, so Mom moved on. I never expected she would start dating a woman. We were walking to the store, and on the way back, she asked me to sit down before we got back to the house. My mom was living with a different friend now…

I do not remember her exact words, but she asked me what I thought of her friend. I had just met this friend recently, but I had noticed that "she" dressed like a boy and even cut her hair like a male. So I told my mom, "She dresses like a boy."

Mom then began to explain how some people are different, like her friend, not only because of how they look, but also because of who they choose to date. This friend of Mom's liked girls. I was surprised, but I did not show any emotion to my mom. After she explained it to me, she asked me what I would think if she was like her friend. Being just 11 years old, I didn't know what to think and definitely didn't know what to say, so I said, "Well, I want you to be happy."

That is true; I do want my mom to be happy. But homosexuality makes me uncomfortable.

I got saved when I was six years old. My grandma and grandpa brought me to church every Sunday and helped lead me to the Lord. I was never told about homosexuals until I had already figured it out on my own. I do not support my mother's view on homosexuality because in the Bible, it is an abomination to God. As a young Christian woman, I want to honor the Lord in all that I do, and I would like my mom to give her life to the Lord. I am continuously praying for her.

I pray for my relationship with my mom. We do have a great relationship in that we can talk to each other about anything. My mom trusts me, and I trust her. My mother's partner and I do not converse. In fact, we hardly associate. She is a nice person with a kind heart, but I still have a hard time dealing with my mother's "marriage." I know holding to Christian values can seem rude and judgmental, but I do not cast down the people who participate in homosexuality. However, there is no compromising God's standard—even for my mom. So when I go to my mom's house, it can seem a little different. I still struggle with how to deal with seeing my mom in a homosexual relationship. Even the simple things like looking in the fridge for something to eat are different at my mom's. At my dad's, I look, grab and eat. But at my mom's, I ask her if it's okay to eat her food. I guess at times I feel more like a guest in her home than family.

Another thing that is different when your mom is in a lesbian relationship is visits. My brother and I go on visits together. I share a room with my two younger brothers. I usually don't use the room though, I just stuff some clothes in a bag and sleep on the couch. I don't bring friends to my mom's, as I want to spend time with her. I never seem to have enough time with just her.

So I am still growing in this situation with my mom. I am not angry with her. I don't treat her differently. Despite the fact I don't have much of a relationship with her partner, I do not disrespect her. Yes, they both know how I feel about the relationship and that I don't support it. But they both also know that I pray for them. I will continue to pray for them. I will always care about their future with the Lord. I do not see myself as better than them. However, I know that it is God's desire for me to bring Him along when I see them.

As I write this, I have finished my sophomore year in high school. At times, I regret not saying something different when my mom told me about her relationship. I do want my mom happy, but even more, I want her to have a relationship with Jesus. At 11, I probably handled it the best way I knew, though I knew homosexuality was not God's best plan for my mom. Please pray with me for my mom and her partner. God loves them. Please pray for me as I am doing my best to be an example for my mom of God's unconditional love without compromise.

—J.V.

Chapter 21

TESTIMONIES OF REDEMPTION

I felt like my life was worthless, that I was born to be used and abused. My first sexual experience happened when I was in the second grade. I was gang raped by five fifth graders. Unfortunately, this act opened the door to many other unwanted sexual acts. I was molested by many males in my family, a pattern that began at age six and would continue until I was 15 years of age.

My young teenage years were difficult as I had a need to feel protected. I was tired of being bullied. I was tired of being made to do things that I did not want to do. So I took on this tough girl image. I wanted people to know that messing with me was not a good idea. It wasn't until high school that people began to tease me about being gay as my demeanor had changed. I looked hard, walked hard, and I had become "Miss Tough Girl." I didn't consider myself a lesbian at that time. However, this is when I began to struggle with keeping my eyes off the girls. I was conflicted. I was the church girl, and yet I was so lost.

During my junior year of high school, my parents divorced. I thought this would make life better at home, but it was worse. The beatings continued, my siblings and I fought more, and we were very violent. This went on for two years. I hated life. I wanted to die; but instead, at the age of 18, I joined the military. Military life was great. I was away from all the nonsense of home, but that deep-rooted unhappiness followed me. All I wanted was to be loved, but I could not find it. After several failed suicide attempts, I thought having a child would help. I began to attend church, but these things only provided temporary enjoyment. I was 21, a single mom, and miserable. This continued for years.

In 2001, I began to spend a lot of time in online chat rooms. I was trying to fill a void. I met a young lady, and over the next year, our relationship blossomed. In 2002, we became a proud lesbian couple. I had found the love that was missing in my life. My girlfriend lived in Canada, so I flew there often. We spent countless hours on the phone. I knew she was the one. About a year later, I decided it was time to pop the question, so I bought a ring, went to Canada, and proposed. I was so excited. This was the best relationship I had ever had with anyone, and I wasn't ever going to let her go. I traveled several times a year to see my fiancé. I fell in love with her family; everything was falling into place. In 2005, my girlfriend came to live with me for eight months. We had a great time together; we went to church, the movies, amusement parks, and more. We also made the decision that we would marry once I retired from the military. Her visit came to an end, and we took the bus back to Canada. Then I caught a flight home.

Just as my life was getting back to normal, one afternoon I was walking to my ship and enjoying the weather when I heard these words, "walk out of it, the same way you walked in." I knew exactly what that meant. I had to walk away from the love of my life. I wasn't sure how I was going to do it, or when, but I knew I had heard God. It took a while, but I made the call to end our relationship. I shed many tears that year; but God gave me the peace and the strength that I needed to continue making steps away from homosexuality. I never turned back. Walking away was super hard, but God sent people to help me. God is still bringing me into new levels of freedom. I thank Him daily for all that He has done and continues to do in and through my life.

—K.J.

Freedom Through the Person, Not the Process

I grew up in a Christian home, the middle of three sons. I not only had a sensitive temperament, but also what is called the middle-child, "notice me" syndrome. Children are the greatest recorders of information but the poorest interpreters and I internalized my family dynamics in a way which became detrimental for me. I felt I was rejected and not truly loved, which I now know was a wrong interpretation. The culpability rests with me.

I began building walls, feeling separate and isolated from my family early in my childhood. I blocked out the love from my parents while at the same time, I yearned for it. I became the good son, caught up in performance-based acceptance. I had no clue who I was and allowed my feelings, behaviors, and others to define me.

As I entered puberty, the legitimate, emotional need I had to be connected with men who could affirm my maleness and masculinity, became eroticized. My isolation deepened. Innately I knew something was wrong, but did not have the language to articulate my turmoil. In 1969, a teacher took me to a Full Gospel Business Men's meeting where I asked Jesus into my heart. I became involved in the Jesus movement but was troubled by my sexual struggles.

In college, I suppressed my struggles and tried walking with the Lord. After college, I could no longer suppress my unwanted same-sex attractions (SSA) and began dating a man. I entered into a six-year relationship with him. When that relationship failed, I became co-dependently involved with another man. He was involved with another man, but our co-dependency kept us sexually bound to each other. After four painful years, I broke up with him. This led to alcohol abuse and several short-term relationships.

In 1986, God sovereignly brought Christians into my path. In August of 1987, I rededicated my life to Jesus, but this time I asked Him to be Lord and not just Savior. I wanted Him to be Lord over my sexuality. In January of 1988, I found out about Regeneration and met with Alan Medinger. I attended my first Regeneration meeting in Northern Virginia in February. What a joy to know of others who were like me, searching for freedom, and to finally hear testimonies.

During those early years, I did everything I could to achieve my "healing." I was driven by restless activism, thinking my process was a checklist. I was in charge, not God. Finally, God broke through, and the Holy Spirit revealed to me that I am not defined by my temptations, feelings, or behaviors. I am defined by who I am in Christ and who Christ is in me. My righteousness is not dependent on my behavioral sobriety but on the reality of Jesus Christ being my identity. It is in Him that I live and move and have my being!

Jesus then led me to the Father. Entering into a greater intimacy with Father God, my inner ache and void became more solid and confident in the man He created me to be! A key part of my process was becoming known in the body of Christ. I developed open and honest friendships with other men. As we became known to one another, I realized most of my struggles were common to men and not based solely on my same-sex attraction. I was just like them, not separate, not different! Becoming more centered in the man God created me to be, my relationships changed with women as well. In due course, I began dating and even pondered marriage as a real possibility.

I am now more than 25 years into my process. I now know trying to find a "cause" for my struggles, although helpful, would not achieve the freedom I sought. My freedom came when I entered into true intimacy with God as Father, my beloved Jesus, and my precious Holy Spirit. My motivation is grounded in my relationship, my love affair with God. It's not a method but a person! I'm not pursuing the healing of my soul but the Healer of my soul. Change and freedom in my life were the byproduct of my deeper relationship with Jesus.

The goal is not healing, change, or victory but becoming who God originally created me to be!

—B.R.

My Personal Story

My name is Davon and I am an overcomer. Although I have had victory over many different types of sin, there was one sin in particular that had a stronghold over my life, but I'm pleased to say I'm finally set free—from homosexuality.

I knew I wasn't born gay. I was attracted to women exclusively until the age of 13. But one sexual encounter in the seventh grade changed that. I was molested—not just by anyone, but by a family relative—a male cousin. Since it was the first time I was exposed to sexual behavior at that level, it was a very uncomfortable experience for me. I was nervous. Traumatized. I felt afraid. Violated. But the consecutive molestations that took place after that began to numb those convictions. After being molested repeatedly from one weekend visit to another, I went from being *turned off*, to being *turned on*, to eventually being *turned out*. I became so conditioned, I even transitioned from being a helpless victim to being a consensual participant during the sex acts.

The molestations weren't the only thing that caused me to develop same-sex desires. Porn addiction played a huge role in fueling my lust for men, as well. Porn subconsciously forced me to pay closer attention to the anatomy of a man—their sturdy stature, their chiseled muscles, their smooth and clean-shaven skin, their oversized genitalia, their charming smiles. I admired the men I saw on the screen and would often compare my body with theirs. Yet, because I wasn't careful to guard my heart, my admiration for these men perverted into an infatuation for them. I began to create fantasies in my mind about the male actors on set. I didn't just want to possess their unique physical qualities—I wanted to possess them, period.

As if being molested by a man and becoming addicted to gay porn wasn't enough, the constant, piercing rejection I received from women my whole life was icing on the cake. That led me further down the path of homosexuality. I was led to believe that I wasn't what women wanted in a man because I didn't have buff muscles, dreads, tattoos, swag, or money. But other men, on the other hand, seemed to accept me more unconditionally. They would call me cute, fine, and sexy through emails. They would offer to take me out on dates, buy nice things for me, and knew how to rub me the right way. They made me feel wanted, accepted, and loved, which boosted my self-esteem carnally, but brought great warfare to me spiritually. I was conflicted in my soul, because I didn't understand how the lifestyle I was indulging in could produce in me both pleasure and guilt at the same time.

Years later, I came to find out that God would not allow me to become fully comfortable in the homosexual lifestyle because that wasn't His original plan for my life. Although I experienced many fun and pleasurable moments during my random affairs with other men, not a single encounter could take away the feelings of guilt, shame, regret, remorse, self-condemnation, hypocrisy, depression, and hopelessness I felt. I was always left feeling unhappy, unsatisfied, and unfulfilled afterward. Soon, the convictions that were numbed out earlier on in my life began to come back even stronger. I wanted to live a guilt-free life again. A life of sexual purity. A life of victory. A life of redemption. A life that glorified God. So I accepted Jesus into my life as my Lord and Savior.

Jesus has since taught me how to find love, identity, purpose, acceptance, affirmation, and forgiveness in Him—not in other people, places, or things. He has helped me to overcome my 10-year addiction to pornography, taught me how to have self-control over my body, and how to say no to sexual advances. Furthermore, He has exchanged my preference for men with a preference for a wife. I am now married as of June 28, 2014, to my virtuous wife, Deborah. I am free. And I'm not going back to bondage.

—**D.J.**

Learning to Live

Hi, my name is Jonathan. I met Janet Boynes about four years ago when I saw JBM in a church bulletin at a church in Maplewood, Minnesota. I contacted Janet, and the rest is history.

I was born and raised in Minnesota and except for a stint in the army, have stuck pretty close to home. I lived in St. Paul. I am the middle child of three sisters. My childhood was spent pretty much getting blamed for everything negative or bad that happened. Before my parents finally divorced in 2001, I lived with my mom. We grew up poor, living on food stamps. My mom did not want anyone to know, so we often shopped when no one else was in the store. I remember eating a lot of buttered noodles and sugar sandwiches growing up. If we were lucky, we had bananas to go with our sandwiches. It was just the way it was. When I graduated, I went into the army.

When I was in junior high, I met a girl named Leann. Later, while on leave from the army over the holidays, we connected again and those brief couple of weeks would change my life—not for the better. After the army, I sort of drifted from one relationship to the next. When relationships with women didn't work out, I got involved with men. Back in the day, being bisexual was considered cool, so it was no big deal. But I found out that relationships with men couldn't fill the void in my life any more than relationships with women could.

In 1998, I got saved. Yeah, pretty cool. It was at Faith Temple Church in the cities. I stayed there for a while and then went to Victory Church and met a man named Michael. He mentored me and showed me a how to have healthy relationships with men.

Then in April 2003, my world changed forever. I was working at a local restaurant and got sick. I chalked it up to food poisoning or something and felt better after a few days. But then one day, I was going up the stairs after doing my laundry and couldn't make it to the top. I eventually made it to the couch but was very weak. My dad came home, took one look at me and said I didn't look good and wanted to call an ambulance. He ended up bringing me to Regions Hospital, and for the next three to four weeks, I was poked and prodded around the clock, but no answers were given as to what was going on. Finally, they called in an infectious disease specialist and he looked at me square in the face and said, "You have HIV/AIDS."

It was then that I truly believe God spoke to me. It was more of a feeling deep down in my gut… time seemed to slow down. The voices in the room seemed to slow to a snail's pace. Even though I was present in the room and everything was going on around me, it felt like it was just me and God. He asked me one question, "What do you want to do? I can take you now and bring you home, or I could let you stay. What do you want to do? I am giving you the choice."

I wanted to get married. I wanted to have kids someday. I wanted to live. I told God I wanted to stay. It was like a light switch was turned on. I instantly felt energy and life pouring into me. You have to understand, I was moments from death. But instead, I was able to get out of bed, and I got better each day. Interestingly enough, about a year after my diagnosis, I got a call from Leann. Remember her? We got to talking and she shared that one of her partners before me had died of AIDS. Then I knew. She had given it to me.

Since my diagnosis and after meeting Janet, I have grown and God has been good. I take medication for my illness and at times, wonder if I will ever marry or have children. But each day is in God's hands. I guess if I had any advice to parents or loved ones who have someone like me in their life, I would ask that you please not rush to judgment. Help your loved ones heal in their hearts. I could be your son—your son with HIV. Help your child heal, encourage him, love him, forgive him, and help him pursue God. Be someone who can be trusted. Be the hands and feet of Jesus. To me. To the world.

−J.V.

Chapter 22

LGBTX!

Today the LGBT (lesbian, gay, bisexual, transgender) movement is increasing in size and influence in our schools, churches and communities. New letters are continually being added to the LGBT acronym as the list of sexual behaviors continues to grow and spiral downward. It's time to add the letter X.

The X represents the ex-gay movement that is growing all across America. Thousands of ex-gays are discovering the mercy and forgiveness that only God can give. They are claiming their God-given identity and experiencing freedom. I know, because I am an ex-gay. I left the homosexual lifestyle and never looked back.

Ex-gays are discovering true fulfillment and purpose after deciding to follow Jesus and His plan for their lives. The X puts an end to the endless possibilities of sexual lifestyles.

So when you use the acronym, be sure to add the X!

Free in Christ,

Janet

Chapter 23

FREQUENTLY ASKED QUESTIONS...

Question: Today the biggest lie in homosexual propaganda is that gays are born that way, and pastors are being pressured to believe this. How do you overcome that falsehood for those people who believe science says it's genetic or an inherent trait that can't be changed? You are living straight, married, and healed from this sin, but how do you address the science that may say you were never born that way, you simply chose to live it for a while as an experiment and returned to your original sexuality. It's my understanding that what studies have been done to prove the born-gay-theory have been investigated and found to be flawed, biased, etc.

Answer: There's no clear scientific evidence that anyone is born gay. If you are hearing this, it is based on lies, not truth. If there was dependable scientific evidence that some people are born gay, I would have no problem accepting it. The truth is, we are all created in God's image, and yet we are a fallen race—all of us carry aspects of that fallen nature and for some that includes homosexuality. Because we live in a fallen, sinful world, sin comes naturally to everybody.

Being born gay has proven so useful to those pushing the gay agenda, that the fact there's no scientific support for the theory hardly matters. It's an idea that has worked wonders for gay activists and their allies who use this as a tool to promote the gay agenda. Tony Perkins, president of the Family Research Council, wrote an article for www.Barbwire.com in which he details the admissions of a leading gay activist:

> If Americans don't want to take our word on the real gay agenda, they can take S. Bear Bergman's. The Canadian activist was shockingly blunt about her movement's motives—which she says she's tired of hiding… "I am here to tell you: All that time I said I wasn't indoctrinating anyone with my beliefs about gay and lesbian and bi and trans and queer people? That was a lie," she wrote in an article for Huffington Post called: "I Have Come to Indoctrinate Your Children into My LGBTQ Agenda (And I'm Not a Bit Sorry)."
>
> The head of a Toronto publishing company, Bergman said she was taught how to use "soft" language when speaking about homosexuality—and not betray the real goal, which was recruiting. "I want kids to know (we're perfectly fine and often really excellent) even if their parents' or community's interpretation of their religious tenets is that we're awful. I would be

happy—delighted, overjoyed I tell you—to cause those children to disagree with their families on the subject of LGBTQ people."

For years, activists wanted to keep the goal of ensnaring children into sexual confusion under wraps. Now, having hoodwinked most of the country on their agenda, these extremists no longer have to hide. In fact, they are increasingly bold—almost boastful—about their real intentions. Although Bergman admits to wanting to "indoctrinate" and "recruit" children, her description of the LGBT agenda is far less honest. "I have been on a consistent campaign of trying to change people's minds about us. I want to make them like us. That is absolutely my goal." (Perkins)

In many areas, science has been reduced to politics instead of being fact-based. In other words, politics is influencing science.

Even though I believe no one is born gay, that doesn't mean that homosexual attractions are not deeply rooted. Some of the feelings are very deeply rooted to the point that homosexuals really believe they were born gay. However, one's personal feelings do not change the facts. Yes, you are entitled to your own feelings, but you are not entitled to your own facts. There is no scientific evidence that anyone is born gay.

Our sexual bodies were designed for reproduction between a man and a woman. We know that two men or two women cannot reproduce. The original intent for sexuality can be found in Genesis. Here God says that a man and woman are to be joined together and become one flesh. Jesus confirmed that marriage structure in Matthew 19 when He said, "For this reason a man shall leave his father and mother and be joined to his wife, and the two shall become one flesh" (v. 5, NKJV). A male and a female fit together beautifully in the marital act; two people of the same sex do not.

The idea of being born gay is unreasonable ... homosexuality is an alteration not an inborn trait. The apostle Paul, in essence, stated that homosexuality is a choice when he said people had "abandoned" and "exchanged" the natural sexual relationship between a man and a woman for homosexual relations (Romans 1:26-27, NASB).

Again, this does not mean that same-sex attractions and desires are not deeply rooted in some people's lives due to rape, abuse, rejection, or a myriad of other reasons. But once we begin to understand God's true plan for our identity, we begin to think in a new way. We no longer feel trapped in bondage to homosexuality. Now our minds are renewed and the old thoughts are being replaced with new thinking. The bottom line is that God loves us right where we are, yet loves us enough to not leave us the same way we came to Him.

Question: What are some things about the homosexual lifestyle that proponents don't want the public to know? What is the dark side of this sin? What are they hiding?

Answer: When I was in that lifestyle, a lot of us didn't truly believe that we were gay. We knew that we had ended up where we were because of life experiences in our past; experiences that truly marked us and were never resolved. There are many who engage in pornography which opens the door to homosexuality. Watching men or women having sex with multiple partners can set one on a path they never intended to take. Many male homosexuals will not admit that indulging in pornography caused them to want to have a relationship with another man.

The homosexual community feels validated in their sin, even to the point that they have the president's support. Hollywood, the media, and a percentage of our population have bought into the lie that homosexuals are born this way. Some teachers are using their classes to tell kids false information about homosexuality. They are trying to put it in the regular classroom curriculum so they don't have to get parents' permission. For a while, the LGBT hid the fact that they were trying to indoctrinate children. Thankfully, their agenda has been discovered and exposed.

When I was in a relationship with a woman, we fought all the time and there was major dysfunction. We were responding out of our own pain. Being in a relationship with a woman didn't solve my identity problems, it enhanced them. We were just trying to hide the fact that there was a deep seed of unhappiness.

Question: Many believe that kids today are only prone to the gay lifestyle if they've been sexually abused by a same-sex adult/peer or have problems at home. The fact is, because homosexuality is now a culturally acceptable behavior, kids are experimenting. Are you hearing and seeing that as well? How can we unite to protect kids from this lie?

Answer: Yes, I have heard of this. This is a very sad reality. The weight of responsibility for talking to our children about this truly rests heavily on the parents. Perhaps many years ago you could get away without talking about homosexuality, but not today. If you aren't discussing this issue with your kids, they will hear about it from friends, other family members, or Gay Straight Alliance (GSA) groups at school. Your kids most likely know more about this issue than you do, so have the conversation with them.

Young people are inquisitive and looking for honest dialogue. Homosexuality can no longer be the elephant in the room; talk about it! Make sure your family is attending a church that still holds the Word of God as the final authority on how to live our lives. Be open, transparent, honest and real; children can see right through us. The pressure to accept homosexuality comes from so many avenues: athletes, politicians, Hollywood, schools and even some churches. Teens who are already dealing with self-doubt and self-worth can be influenced by people they respect.

Churches must take a loving, but bold stand. First Corinthians 14:8 says, "If the trumpet call can't be distinguished, will anyone show up for the battle?" (MSG). Our churches must take a firm stand on the truth so Christians do not become deceived.

Question: What are the worst things a pastor can do about this issue? Not address it at all? Be uneducated about the problem? Kick these hurting folks out of the church?

Answer: I think there are several things that have harmed the Church's influence when it comes to addressing the elephant in the room. The biggest mistake is when a pastor decides to make a statement based on his opinions or feeling rather than what the Word says. If a pastor is bashing, criticizing, and running those who struggle with homosexuality out of his church, he or she is clearly not acting out of love. If a pastor says that it is acceptable to God to live a life of homosexuality, that too is not acting out of love. The pastor who is gay bashing is pushing people out of the church so he does not have to deal with them, and the pastor who is accepting of homosexuality is following modern culture rather than Scripture, perhaps seeking acceptance himself.

Remember, when you know better, you do better. Becoming knowledgeable on this topic is crucial if your heart is truly focused on seeing those in this lifestyle become whole and walk in holiness. My heart's desire is the same as the Lord's: He wants all people to be saved and to come to a knowledge of the truth (1 Timothy 2:4).

The Church is and always has been for those who need a doctor: "On hearing this, Jesus said to them, 'It is not the healthy who need a doctor, but the sick. I have not come to call the righteous, but sinners'" (Mark 2:17, NIV). You can help those who are struggling by meeting their real need and loving them in a healthy way. This is where you need to step up, even when you're uncomfortable. Reach out to young men who are struggling with homosexuality. They need to receive support from a male figure. This can be hard because there are many homosexuals who will say, "If you don't embrace my behavior, then you don't love me." You have to find a way to break through that wall. You can say, "No, I won't stop believing there's something better for you. But even if you don't believe that, I really want to be there to help you."

Question: What can pastors do to address this issue in their church? Are there educational presentations, reading materials, support groups for those who struggle with same-sex attraction? Should they hire a counselor who specializes in this?

Answer: I encourage pastors to be bold and address homosexuality from the pulpit in a compassionate way without compromising God's Word. Pastors have to do their own research so when the time comes to bring in special counsel to help the church, the person they hire will be aligned with God's Word. What you are doing when you research homosexuality ahead of time is being proactive instead of reactive. It also helps to bring in speakers who have overcome same-sex attraction and have a message of hope and redemption.

It is important that for people who want help, there are those on staff who are equipped and willing to walk this journey with them. The Bible says, "Refuse good advice and watch your plan fail, take good counsel and watch them succeed" (Proverbs 15:22, MSG). It requires time and commitment to help someone who truly wants to be set free. In my case, it went as far as moving in with a family from church for a year. If you are an empty nester, why not bring a single person into your home? In my ministry, I work with pastors and churches on how to assist someone who wants out of that lifestyle.

Please email our ministry, and we will work together in assisting in any way we can.

Question: Many pastors are afraid to address this issue from the pulpit because they fear retaliation from the gay community. They fear that their freedom to speak of this as a sin will soon be punishable by fines, loss of tax exemption, etc. What would you say to encourage them to talk about this openly, and can you set the record straight on their legal religious and free speech rights?

Answer: When God's love is what motivates your message, then fear has no place in it. If eternity is our main focus and not how much money we receive, then we must speak the truth in love.

The gay community will come against us sooner or later. The question is: Will you be found standing or will you be found ducking behind your pulpit? Yes, they are trying to silence the faith-based community. But they don't give us our marching orders, only God does through His Word. The apostle Paul said that if he were seeking to please men, then he would not be a bondservant of God (Galatians 1:10). We must stand up for the truth, regardless of what people think.

Churches and religious organizations must now face the issues of same-sex marriage and acceptance of multiple genders. Our churches are faced with requests to use their facilities for same-sex ceremonies in direct violation of church beliefs. Our Christian schools are being asked to employ persons who identify as transgender, gay, or lesbian. It is important that churches, Christian schools and Christian ministries develop a clear statement on marriage, gender, and sexuality within their statements of faith. This statement will help protect religious organizations, and it may discourage those looking to bring claims for "easy" lawsuits. Once an organization clearly states its religious beliefs on these matters, it is more difficult to argue that the organization acted with improper motives. Adopting a statement of faith makes it more likely a court will conclude the organization acted on its well-documented and sincere religious beliefs. The statement will make it easier for the organization to defend itself if it is sued.

Courts generally regard a clear statement of faith as an expression of the organization's doctrine, and defer to it as protected by the First Amendment. Remember, this statement is not intended to limit the organization's ability to reach or serve a particular group, but rather to protect it from being forced to operate in a way that violates its religious beliefs. It will be impossible to anticipate every doctrinal dispute that a church, Christian school, or Christian ministry might encounter. New disputes arise regularly, and it is important that pastors are able to respond in a legally defensible way.

We could not have imagined decades ago, when many of the existing church creeds and statements of faith were written, that marriage would be anything but the union of a man and a woman. No one could foresee that many would not only advocate for marriage redefinition, but also demand that churches host same-sex ceremonies. Consequently, pastors were not prepared when this cultural war broke out.

I believe every Christian organization should have a statement that clearly identifies both the source of religious authority for matters of faith and conduct and the final human interpreter of that source for the organization. Such a statement should cover unforeseeable threats that might arise in the future.

Question: You have a helpline listed on your website. Can you please tell me more about that? Who is providing the help (are they former homosexuals, are they licensed/ordained in Christian counseling, etc.)? Do callers get connected with a local support group, receive materials to read, etc.?

Answer: Yes, we do have a helpline. The majority of the time, I make the initial call to whomever has reached out to the ministry. Depending on their needs, I determine if I will continue to guide them spiritually or if someone from my team will. I have two Oral Robert University graduates who do most of the mentoring and I also have someone who has come out of that lifestyle who helps as well. We are not licensed counselors and we have never claimed to be. We are spiritual leaders who are ready and able to invest our time and efforts in helping with whatever people are going through. If there is a local support group that we are familiar with, we definitely connect them with that group. We believe in the wonderful work of the local church and local communities who take on the role of mentors and even become a family to those who want the help.

Disclaimer: The material available in this chapter is for informational purposes only and not for the purpose of providing legal advice. You should contact your attorney to obtain advice with respect to any particular issue or problem.

STUDY GUIDE AND DISCUSSION QUESTIONS

Chapter 1 Did God Make Me This Way?

1. What contributes to a person's belief system? (See page 11.)
   a. Societal factors
   b. Environmental factors
   c. Biblical factors
   d. All of the above

2. Read Jeremiah 1:5. Did God know us before He created us? Does God know who He created us to be? (See page 11.)

3. Where do we find God's blueprint for the world before sin entered into the world? (See page 11.)

4. Read Genesis 1:27-28. What one pairing allows mankind to be fruitful and multiply? (See page 12.)

5. What is the purpose of God for male and female according to Matthew 19:4-6 and Ephesians 5:31? (See pages 12-13.)

6. Read Matthew 19:4-6 and Ephesians 5:31. What type of relationship is being promoted through marriage? (See page 13.)

7. Read Romans 1:20-32. Where did homosexuality come from? (See page 13.)?

8. Why did God allow homosexuality? (See page 15.)

9. Read Romans 10:9-10, 1 Timothy 2:4 and John 3:16. What are the qualifications for approaching God to be forgiven of all sins and receiving salvation through Jesus? (See page 15.)

10. What is the real solution to healing and wholeness in life? (See pages 15-16.)

Answer Key for Chapter 1 Discussion Questions

1. d. All of the above (See page 11.)

2. Yes (See page 11.)

3. Creation story in Genesis (See page 11.)

4. Heterosexual, male and female (See page 12.)

5. For the male and female to join/unite in marriage and be one (See pages 12-13.)

6. Between male and female (See page 13.)

7. Sinful desires, sin nature (See page 13.)

8. Because people turned the truth into a lie and rejected God's truth in their hearts (See page 15.)

9. No qualification, all people, anyone, whosoever (See page 15.)

10. Jesus or having a relationship with Jesus (See pages 15-16.)

Scripture References Chapter 1

JEREMIAH 1:5 MSG

Before I shaped you in the womb, I knew all about you. Before you saw the light of day, I had holy plans for you: A prophet to the nations—that's what I had in mind for you.

GENESIS 1:27-28 NIV

So God created mankind in his own image, in the image of God he created them; male and female he created them. God blessed them and said to them, "Be fruitful and increase in number; fill the earth and subdue it. Rule over the fish in the sea and the birds in the sky and over every living creature that moves on the ground."

MATTHEW 19:4-6 NIV

"Haven't you read," he replied, "that at the beginning the Creator 'made them male and female,' and said, 'For this reason a man will leave his father and mother and be united to his wife, and the two will become one flesh'? So they are no longer two, but one flesh. Therefore what God has joined together, let no one separate."

EPHESIANS 5:31 NIV

For this reason a man will leave his father and mother and be united to his wife, and the two will become one flesh.

ROMANS 1:20-32 MSG

But God's angry displeasure erupts as acts of human mistrust and wrongdoing and lying accumulate, as people try to put a shroud over truth. But the basic reality of God is plain enough. Open your eyes and there it is! By taking a long and thoughtful look at what God has created, people have always been able to see what their eyes as such can't see: eternal power, for instance, and the mystery of his divine being. So nobody has a good excuse. What happened was this: People knew God perfectly well, but when they didn't treat him like God, refusing to worship him, they trivialized themselves into silliness and confusion so that there was neither sense nor direction left in their lives. They pretended to know it all, but were illiterate regarding life. They traded the glory of God who holds the whole world in his hands for cheap figurines you can buy at any roadside stand.

So God said, in effect, "If that's what you want, that's what you get." It wasn't long before they were living in a pigpen, smeared with filth, filthy inside and out. And all this because they traded the true God for a fake god, and worshiped the god they made instead of the God who made them—the God we bless, the God who blesses us. Oh, yes!

Worse followed. Refusing to know God, they soon didn't know how to be human either—women didn't know how to be women, men didn't know how to be men. Sexually confused, they abused and defiled one another, women with women, men with men—all lust, no love. And then they paid for it, oh, how they paid for it—emptied of God and love, godless and loveless wretches.

Since they didn't bother to acknowledge God, God quit bothering them and let them run loose. And then all hell broke loose: rampant evil, grabbing and grasping, vicious backstabbing. They made life hell on earth with their envy, wanton killing, bickering, and cheating. Look at them: mean-spirited, venomous, fork-tongued God-bashers. Bullies, swaggerers, insufferable windbags! They keep inventing new ways of wrecking lives. They ditch their parents when they get in the way. Stupid, slimy, cruel, cold-blooded. And it's not as if they don't know better. They know perfectly well they're spitting in God's face. And they don't care—worse, they hand out prizes to those who do the worst things best!

ROMANS 10:9-10 NIV

If you declare with your mouth, "Jesus is Lord," and believe in your heart that God raised him from the dead, you will be saved. For it is with your heart that you believe and are justified, and it is with your mouth that you profess your faith and are saved.

1 TIMOTHY 2:4 NIV

…who wants all people to be saved and to come to a knowledge of the truth.

JOHN 3:16 NIV

For God so loved the world that he gave his one and only Son, that whoever believes in him shall not perish but have eternal life.

Chapter 2 I Want You To Support Me

1. What kind of basic needs does every human being have? (See page 17.)
    a. Physical - food, water, air
    b. Emotional - validation, security, approval

c. All of the above

d. None of the above

2. Read Exodus 20:12. Should parents allow children to disrespect them? (See page 18.)

3. Read Matthew 3:17. Who is being validated by whom? Who is beloved by Whom? (See page 18.)

4. Is acceptance the same as approval? (See page 18.)

5. Can a parent love their rebellious child without compromising the gospel of Jesus? (See page 18.)

6. Can a parent love their gay child without compromising the Bible? (See page 18.)

7. Read Proverbs 22:6. What are the parents told to do? (See page 19.)

8. Is it possible to love your child despite the child's poor choices? (See page 19.)

9. Is it possible to validate a gay person without agreeing of condoning their lifestyle? (See page 19.)

10. What is one of the important steps to take before praying for the children that are choosing gay lifestyle? (See page 19.)

11. What does forgiveness help us with? (See pages 19-20.)

a. Sets us free to move and flow in our prayers

b. Establishes the foundation to be kind and compassionate

c. Both a and b

d. None of the above

Answer Key for Chapter 2 Discussion Questions

1. c. All of the above (See page 17.)

2. No (See page 18.)

3. Jesus is being validated by God; Jesus is God's beloved Son (See page 18.)

4. No (See page 18.)

5. Yes (See page 18.)

6. Yes (See page 18.)

7. Train the child (in keeping with their individual gift) (See page 19.)

8. Yes (See page 19.)

9. Yes (See page 19.)

10. Forgive them (See page 19.)

11. c. Both a and b (See pages 19-20.)

Scripture References Chapter 2

EXODUS 20:12 NIV

Honor your father and your mother, so that you may live long in the land the LORD your God is giving you.

MATTHEW 3:17 NLT

And a voice from heaven said, "This is my dearly loved Son, who brings me great joy."

PROVERBS 22:6 AMPC

Train up a child in the way he should go [and in keeping with his individual gift or bent], and when he is old he will not depart from it.

Chapter 3 Can I Still Be a Christian and Be Gay?

1. What are some of the voices we hear today in our culture? List a few. (See page 21.)
   a. Media, movies
   b. Political system
   c. Educational system
   d. Religious system

2. Read Ephesians 4:14. Can people trick and deceive other people? Can people teach and give advice lacking biblical truth? (See page 21.)

3. Read Leviticus 18:22, 1 Corinthians 6:9-11, and 1 Timothy 1:8-10. Does the Bible seem to be clear that homosexuality is a sin? (See page 22.)

4. Read 2 Peter 3:16. Is it possible to twist and manipulate scripture? (See page 22.)

5. Read Galatians 1:7-8. Are there different/alternative gospels? (See page 22.)

6. Can the truth change or fluctuate?

7. Read Galatians 1:10. What are the 2 options mentioned? (See page 22.)

8. Read Romans 12:2. What are we told to do in relation to pattern of this world?

9. Read Romans 1:25. What did the people exchange the truth for? (See page 23.)

10. Read Genesis 18:20-21 and Genesis 19:1-12. What kind of sin was the primary sin in Sodom and Gomorra? (See pages 23-24.)

11. According to the Genesis 18 and 19 scriptures referenced above. Was God in favor of homosexuality? (See page 24.)

12. Read Leviticus 18:22. What is clearly forbidden? (See page 24.)

13. Read Genesis 2:24. What is a man to do? Who does a man unite with? (See page 24.)

14. Read 1 Corinthians 7:1-9. What type of sexual relations are discussed here? (See page 25.)

15. What type of sexual relations are not discussed in 1 Corinthians 7 at all? (See page 25.)

16. Read 1 Corinthians 6:9-10. What type of sins are listed that will not inherit the Kingdom of God? (See page 25.)

17. Is being tempted to sin considered sin? (See page 25.)

18. Read Hebrews 4:15. Is it possible to be tempted and not sin? (See pages 25-26.)

19. Read Psalm 119:11. How can a Christian be victorious over sin? (See page 26.)

20. Read Matthew 4:1-11. How did Jesus fight temptation? (See page 26.)

21. Read 1 Corinthians 15:33, 2 Corinthians 6:14 and Proverbs 13:20. According to these verses, is it important to cut off ungodly, bad friendships? (See page 27.)

22. Read Luke 22:40. What is the instruction given to do to not get tempted? (See page 27.)

23. Read Romans 6:1-7 and Titus 2:11-12. Should we continue living in sin and ungodliness? (See pages 27-28.)

24. Read Hebrews 3:13. What does God want us to do?

25. Read Genesis 3:2-4, John 8:44 and 2 Corinthians 11:3. What is one of the most common devil's tactics?

26. Read Hebrews 12:1. What are we to do with sin? (See page 29.)

Answer Key for Chapter 3 Discussion Questions

1. a. Media, movies

    b. Political system

    c. Educational system

    d. Religious system

2. Yes (See page 21.)

3. Yes (See page 22.)

4. Yes (See page 22.)

5. No (See page 22.)

6. No

7. Win approval from/please men or please God (See page 22.)

8. Do not be conformed to the pattern of this world

9. A lie (See page 23.)

10. Homosexuality (See pages 23-24.)

11. No (See page 24.)

12. Homosexuality (See page 24.)

13. A man is to leave father and mother and to unite with his wife (See page 24.)

14. Between a man and a woman (See page 25.)

15. Homosexual (See page 25.)

16. Sexually immoral, idolaters, adulterers, men who have sex with men, thieves, the greedy, drunkards, slanderers, swindlers (See page 25.)

17. No (See page 25.)

18. Yes (See pages 25-26.)

19. By hiding God's word in the heart (See page 26.)

20. With the word of God (See page 26.)

21. Yes (See page 27.)

22. To pray (See page 27.)

23. Not at all (See pages 27-28.)

24. Encourage each other daily so that sin doesn't harden our hearts to God

25. Deception, lying, cunning

26. We are to throw it off or lay it aside (See page 29.)

Scripture References Chapter 3

EPHESIANS **4:14 NIV**

Then we will no longer be infants, tossed back and forth by the waves, and blown here and there by every wind of teaching and by the cunning and craftiness of people in their deceitful scheming.

LEVITICUS **18:22 NIV**

Do not have sexual relations with a man as one does with a woman; that is detestable.

1 CORINTHIANS **6:9-11 NIV**

Or do you not know that wrongdoers will not inherit the kingdom of God? Do not be deceived: Neither the sexually immoral nor idolaters nor adulterers nor men who have sex with men nor thieves nor the greedy nor drunkards nor slanderers nor swindlers will inherit the kingdom of God. And that is what some of you were. But you were washed, you were sanctified, you were justified in the name of the Lord Jesus Christ and by the Spirit of our God.

1 TIMOTHY **1:8-10 NIV**

We know that the law is good if one uses it properly. We also know that the law is made not for the righteous but for lawbreakers and rebels, the ungodly and sinful, the unholy and irreligious, for those who kill their fathers or mothers, for murderers, for the sexually immoral, for those practicing homosexuality, for slave traders and liars and perjurers—and for whatever else is contrary to the sound doctrine

2 PETER **3:16 NLT**

Speaking of these things in all of his letters. Some of his comments are hard to understand, and those who are ignorant and unstable have twisted his letters to mean something quite different, just as they do with other parts of Scripture. And this will result in their destruction.

GALATIANS 1:7-8 ESV

Not that there is another one, but there are some who trouble you and want to distort the gospel of Christ. But even if we or an angel from heaven should preach to you a gospel contrary to the one we preached to you, let him be accursed.

GALATIANS 1:10 NIV

Am I now trying to win the approval of human beings, or of God? Or am I trying to please people? If I were still trying to please people, I would not be a servant of Christ.

ROMANS 12:2 NIV

Do not conform to the pattern of this world, but be transformed by the renewing of your mind. Then you will be able to test and approve what God's will is—his good, pleasing and perfect will.

ROMANS 1:25 NIV

They exchanged the truth about God for a lie, and worshiped and served created things rather than the Creator—who is forever praised. Amen.

GENESIS 18:20-21 NIV

Then the Lord said, "The outcry against Sodom and Gomorrah is so great and their sin so grievous that I will go down and see if what they have done is as bad as the outcry that has reached me. If not, I will know."

GENESIS 2:24 NIV

That is why a man leaves his father and mother and is united to his wife, and they become one flesh.

1 CORINTHIANS 7:1-9 NIV

Now for the matters you wrote about: "It is good for a man not to have sexual relations with a woman." But since sexual immorality is occurring, each man should have sexual relations with his own wife, and each woman with her own husband. The husband should fulfill his marital duty to his wife, and likewise the wife to her husband. The wife does not have authority over her own body but yields it to her husband. In the same way, the husband does not have authority over his own body but yields it to his wife. Do not deprive each other except perhaps by mutual consent and for a time, so that you may devote yourselves to prayer. Then come together again so that Satan will not tempt you because of your lack of self-control. I say this as a concession, not as a command. I wish that all of you were as I am. But each of you has your own gift from God; one has this gift, another has that. Now to the unmarried and the widows I say: It is good for them to stay unmarried, as I do. But if they cannot control themselves, they should marry, for it is better to marry than to burn with passion.

HEBREWS 4:15 NIV

For we do not have a high priest who is unable to empathize with our weaknesses, but we have one who has been tempted in every way, just as we are—yet he did not sin.

PSALM 119:11 NIV

I have hidden your word in my heart that I might not sin against you.

MATTHEW 4:1-11 NIV

Then Jesus was led by the Spirit into the wilderness to be tempted by the devil. After fasting forty days and forty nights, he was hungry. The tempter came to him and said, "If you are the Son of God, tell these stones to become bread." Jesus answered, "It is written: 'Man shall not live on bread alone, but on every word that comes from the mouth of God.'" Then the devil took him to the holy city and had him stand on the highest point of the temple. "If you are the Son of God," he said, "throw yourself down. For it is written: 'He will command his angels concerning you, and they will lift you up in their hands, so that you will not strike your foot against a stone.'" Jesus answered him, "It is also written: 'Do not put the Lord your God to the test.'" Again, the devil took him to a very high mountain and showed him all the kingdoms of the world and their splendor. "All this I will give you," he said, "if you will bow down and worship me." Jesus said to him, "Away from me, Satan! For it is written: 'Worship the Lord your God, and serve him only.'" Then the devil left him, and angels came and attended him.

1 CORINTHIANS 15:33 NIV

Do not be misled: "Bad company corrupts good character."

2 CORINTHIANS 6:14 NIV

Do not be yoked together with unbelievers. For what do righteousness and wickedness have in common? Or what fellowship can light have with darkness?

PROVERBS 13:20 NIV

Walk with the wise and become wise, for a companion of fools suffers harm.

LUKE 22:40 NIV

On reaching the place, he said to them, "Pray that you will not fall into temptation."

ROMANS 6:1-7 NIV

What shall we say, then? Shall we go on sinning so that grace may increase? By no means! We are those who have died to sin; how can we live in it any longer? Or don't you know that all of us who were baptized into Christ Jesus were baptized into his death? We were therefore buried with him through baptism into death in order that, just as Christ was raised from the dead through the glory of the Father, we too may live a new life. For if we have been united with him in a death like his, we will certainly also be united with him in a resurrection like his. For we know that our old self was crucified with him so that the body ruled by sin might be done away with, that we should no longer be slaves to sin—because anyone who has died has been set free from sin.

TITUS 2:11-12 NIV

For the grace of God has appeared that offers salvation to all people. it teaches us to say "No" to ungodliness and worldly passions, and to live self-controlled, upright and godly lives in this present age.

HEBREWS 3:13 NIV

But encourage one another daily, as long as it is called "Today," so that none of you may be hardened by sin's deceitfulness.

GENESIS 3:2-4 NIV

The woman said to the serpent, "We may eat fruit from the trees in the garden, but God did say, 'You must not eat fruit from the tree that is in the middle of the garden, and you must not touch it, or you will die.'" "You will not certainly die," the serpent said to the woman.

JOHN 8:44 NIV

You belong to your father, the devil, and you want to carry out your father's desires. He was a murderer from the beginning, not holding to the truth, for there is no truth in him. When he lies, he speaks his native language, for he is a liar and the father of lies.

2 CORINTHIANS 11:3 NIV

But I am afraid that just as Eve was deceived by the serpent's cunning, your minds may somehow be led astray from your sincere and pure devotion to Christ.

HEBREWS 12:1 NIV

Therefore, since we are surrounded by such a great cloud of witnesses, let us throw off everything that hinders and the sin that so easily entangles. And let us run with perseverance the race marked out for us.

Chapter 4 Becoming An Overcomer

1. Is struggle with sin/temptation from God? (See page 31.)
2. Is struggle with sin/temptation a sign of anger from God? (See page 31.)

3. Is struggle with sin/temptation a curse or punishment for something you did or didn't do? (See page 31.)

4. Read Matthew 11:28-30. What is Jesus promising you if you come to Him? (See page 32.)

   a. Recover your life

   b. Show you how to take a real rest

   c. Learn to live freely and lightly

   d. All the above

5. Are we designed to live apart from God? (See page 32.)

6. Read Romans 7:17-25. How can we overcome sin/temptation? (See page 33.)

7. What are the keys to walking in complete victory over sin, emotions, fleshly struggles? (See page 34.)

   a. Agreeing with Jesus

   b. Reinforcing sin's defeat in our lives

   c. Pay more money to the church

   d. A and B

8. How do we use the keys to walking in compete victory over sin, emotions, fleshly struggles? (See page 34.)

   a. We try really hard to make it work

   b. Cry out to God louder than before

   c. Focus on, meditate and speak God's word

9. Read Matthew 4:1-11. How did Jesus respond to the devil tempting Him? (See page 34.)

10. Read Ephesians 6:10-18. What is the spiritual weapon that is at our disposal? (See page 34.)

11. Read Ephesians 6:17. What are we to do with the sword? (See page 34.)

12. Read Colossians 2:15. What did Jesus do to the spiritual rulers and authorities?

13. Read Mark 11:23. What does Jesus command you to do? (See page 35.)

14. Read the story of Naaman in 2 Kings 5:7-14. Was it easy for Naaman to obey the prophet of God? (See pages 35-37.)

Choose True or False for questions 15-20

15. God is not interested in behavior modification. (See page 37.) _ True _ False

16. God wants you to surrender your struggle to Him. _ True _ False

17. God's healing takes place inside out. (See page 37.) _ True _ False

18. Pride can hinder receiving healing from God. (See page 37.) _ True _ False

19. God wants you to trust Him to carry you through. (See page 37.) _ True _ False

20. God is interested in your transformation and healing. (See page 37.) _ True _ False

Answer Key for Chapter 4 Discussion Questions

1. No (See page 31.)

2. No (See page 31.)

3. No (See page 31.)

4. d. All of the above (See page 32.)

5. No (See page 32.)

6. With Jesus' help (See page 33.)

7. d. A and B (See page 34.)

8. c. Focus on, meditate and speak God's word. (See page 34.)

9. Jesus responded with Scriptures. (See page 34.)

10. The sword of the Spirit which is the word of God. (See page 34.)

11. We are to take it up, we are to use it. (See page 34.)

12. He disarmed them, defeated them.

13. Speak to the mountain (See page 35.)

14. No, it wasn't (See pages 35-37.)

15. True (See page 37.)

16. True

17. True (See page 37.)

18. True (See page 37.)

19. True (See page 37.)

20. True (See page 37.)

Scripture References Chapter 4

MATTHEW 11:28-30 MSG

Are you tired? Worn out? Burned out on religion? Come to me. Get away with me and you'll recover your life. I'll show you how to take a real rest. Walk with me and work with me—watch how I do it. Learn the unforced rhythms of grace. I won't lay anything heavy or ill-fitting on you. Keep company with me and you'll learn to live freely and lightly.

ROMANS 7:17-25 MSG

But I need something more! For if I know the law but still can't keep it, and if the power of sin within me keeps sabotaging my best intentions, I obviously need help! I realize that I don't have what it takes. I can will it, but I can't do it. I decide to do good, but I don't really do it; I decide not to do bad, but then I do it anyway. My decisions, such as they are, don't result in actions. Something has gone wrong deep within me and gets the better of me every time. It happens so regularly that it's predictable. The moment I decide to do good, sin is there to trip me up. I truly delight in God's commands, but it's pretty obvious that not all of me joins in that delight. Parts of me covertly rebel, and just when I least expect it, they take charge. I've tried everything and nothing helps. I'm at the end of my rope. Is there no one who can do anything for me? Isn't that the real question? The answer, thank God, is that Jesus Christ can and does. He acted to set things right in this life of contradictions where I want to serve God with all my heart and mind, but am pulled by the influence of sin to do something totally different.

MATTHEW 4:1-11 NIV

Then Jesus was led by the Spirit into the wilderness to be tempted by the devil. After fasting forty days and forty nights, he was hungry. The tempter came to him and said, "If you are the Son of God, tell these stones to become bread." Jesus answered, "It is written: 'Man shall not live on bread alone, but on every word that comes from the mouth of God.'" Then the devil took him to the holy city and had him stand on the highest point of the temple. "If you are the Son of God," he said, "throw yourself down. For it is written: 'He will command his angels concerning you, and they will lift you up in their hands, so that you will not strike your foot against a stone.'" Jesus answered him, "It is also written: 'Do not put the Lord your God to the test.'" Again, the devil took him to a very high mountain and showed him all the kingdoms of the world and their splendor. "All this I will give you," he said, "if you will bow down and worship me." Jesus said to him, "Away from me, Satan! For it is written: 'Worship the Lord your God, and serve him only.'" Then the devil left him, and angels came and attended him.

EPHESIANS 6:10-18 NIV

Finally, be strong in the Lord and in his mighty power. Put on the full armor of God, so that you can take your stand against the devil's schemes. For our struggle is not against flesh and blood, but against the rulers, against the authorities, against the powers of this dark world and against the spiritual forces of evil in the heavenly realms. Therefore put on the full armor of God, so that when the day of evil comes, you may be able to stand your ground, and after you have done everything, to stand. Stand firm then, with the belt of truth buckled around your waist, with the breastplate of righteousness in place, and with your feet fitted with the readiness that comes from the gospel of peace. In addition to all this, take up the shield of faith, with which you can extinguish all the flaming arrows of the evil one. Take the helmet of salvation and the sword of the Spirit, which is the word of God. And pray in the Spirit on all occasions with all kinds of prayers and requests. With this in mind, be alert and always keep on praying for all the Lord's people.

EPHESIANS 6:17 NIV

Take the helmet of salvation and the sword of the Spirit, which is the word of God.

COLOSSIANS 2:15 NIV

And having disarmed the powers and authorities, he made a public spectacle of them, triumphing over them by the cross.

MARK 11:23 NIV

Truly I tell you, if anyone says to this mountain, "Go, throw yourself into the sea," and does not doubt in their heart but believes that what they say will happen, it will be done for them.

2 KINGS 5:7-14 NLT

When the king of Israel read the letter, he tore his clothes in dismay and said, "Am I God, that I can give life and take it away? Why is this man asking me to heal someone with leprosy? I can see that he's just trying to pick a fight with me." But when Elisha, the man of God, heard that the king of Israel had torn his clothes in dismay, he sent this message to him: "Why are you so upset? Send Naaman to me, and he will learn that there is a true prophet here in Israel." So Naaman went with his horses and chariots and waited at the door of Elisha's house. But Elisha sent a messenger out to him with this message: "Go and wash yourself seven times in the Jordan River. Then your skin will be restored, and you will *be healed of your leprosy." But Naaman became angry and stalked away. "I thought he would certainly come out to meet me!" he said. "I expected him to wave his hand over the leprosy and call on the name of the Lord his God and heal me! Aren't the rivers of Damascus, the Abana and the Pharpar, better than any of the rivers of Israel? Why shouldn't I wash in them and be healed?" So Naaman turned and went away in a rage. But his officers tried to reason with him and said, "Sir, if the prophet had told you to do something very difficult, wouldn't you have done it? So you should certainly obey him when he says simply, 'Go and wash and be cured!'" So Naaman went down to the Jordan River and dipped himself seven times, as the man of God had instructed him. And his skin became as healthy as the skin of a young child, and he was healed!*

Chapter 5 Dialogue with Your Child About His or Her Lifestyle Choice

1. Is open communication important to have with your children? (See page 39.)

2. Read Hebrews 4:15. This is talking about Jesus. Was Jesus tempted? Did Jesus sin?

3. Is temptation to act on same-sex attraction a sin?

4. Read James 1:14-15. Should temptation be dealt with or left alone to progress?

5. Is committing a homosexual act based on desires for the same sex sin?

6. Is committing to a homosexual lifestyle a sin? (See page 40.)

7. What is the key factor in helping your child who is struggling with homosexuality? (See page 41.)

8. Does Jesus love the homosexual? (See page 42.)

9. What must Christians do to protect the hearts and minds of children from false teaching and indoctrination on homosexuality? (See pages 42-43.)

10. Do you think that parenting requires wisdom and discernment? Why?

Answer Key for Chapter 5 Discussion Questions

1. Yes (See page 39.)

2. Yes, but Jesus didn't sin

3. No, it is a feeling, a thought, a flesh desire that should be surrendered over to God

4. Temptation should be dealt with before it turns into sin

5. Yes

6. Yes and it is rebellion to God (See page 40.)

7. Discovering what the Bible teaching about it, taking a child on a journey through scripture that reveals that homosexuality is a sin (See page 41.)

8. Yes (See page 42.)

9. Everything we can possible (See pages 42-43.)

10. Yes, parenting requires wisdom and discernment.

Scripture References Chapter 5

HEBREWS 4:15 NIV

For we do not have a high priest who is unable to empathize with our weaknesses, but we have one who has been tempted in every way, just as we are—yet he did not sin.

JAMES 1:14-15 NIV

...but each person is tempted when they are dragged away by their own evil desire and enticed. Then, after desire has conceived, it gives birth to sin; and sin, when it is full-grown, gives birth to death.

Chapter 6 Know Your Enemy

1. What does traditional family look like that represents the basic foundation in every society? (See page 47.)

2. Read John 10:10. Who is the thief and what is the thief's role? (See page 47.)

3. Has America increasingly experienced a decline in family structure? (See page 48.)

4. Has America increasingly experienced consequences of a declining family structure? (See page 48.)

5. Read 2 Timothy 3:1-5. Can you see these things happening now in our society? (See page 49.)

6. How is the Church supposed to react to the people living in these lifestyles? (See page 49.)

7. What should the Church be teaching about marriage? (See page 49.)

8. How should the Church be teaching these truths? (See page 49.)

9. Are men and women exactly the same? (See pages 49-50.)

10. Is a same-sex household good for a child to grow up in? (See page 50.)

11. Does the homosexual movement have an agenda? (See pages 51-52.)

12. What are the Christians to do in light of the homosexual agenda? (See page 52.)
    a. Christians must speak truth in love
    b. Christians should not compromise on this topic
    c. Be the salt and light to the world
    d. Guard themselves from the temptations of the culture
    e. All of the above

Answer Key for Chapter 6 Discussion Questions

1. Male father, female mother, children (See page 47.)

2. The devil is the thief and his role is to steal, kill and destroy (See page 47.)

3. Yes (See page 48.)

4. Yes (See page 48.)

5. Yes (See page 49.)

6. Church must extend grace and forgiveness (See page 49.)

7. What the Bible says about marriage (See page 49.)

8. With compassion, without condemnation and hate (See page 49.)

9. No (See pages 49-50.)

10. No, a child needs both, a male father and a female mother. (See page 50.)

11. Yes (See pages 51-52.)

12. e. All of the above (See page 52.)

Scripture References Chapter 6

JOHN 10:10 NIV

The thief comes only to steal and kill and destroy; I have come that they may have life, and have it to the full.

2 TIMOTHY 3:1-5 NIV

But mark this: There will be terrible times in the last days. People will be lovers of themselves, lovers of money, boastful, proud, abusive, disobedient to their parents, ungrateful, unholy, without love, unforgiving, slanderous, without self-control, brutal, not lovers of the good, treacherous, rash, conceited, lovers of pleasure rather than lovers of God—having a form of godliness but denying its power. Have nothing to do with such people.

Chapter 7 The Blame Game

1. According to chapter 7, what is vital in a husband and wife relationship when it comes to dealing with stressful situations like a child struggling with sexuality? (See page 53.)

2. What is one hurdle that must be overcome by the spouses? (See page 54.)

3. Read 1 Timothy 4:16, what is Timothy instructed to do by Paul? (See page 54.)

4. Is it important how you approach your spouse about the child's sexuality? (See pages 54-55.)

5. What are the men (dads, husbands) instructed to do in chapter 7? (See page 55.)

6. What is the key to seeing a change you desire in yourself and others? (See page 55.)

7. What are the women (mothers, wives) instructed to do in chapter 7? (See pages 56-57.)

8. How can we change our families? (See page 57.)

9. Read 1 Peter 3:8-9. What are the commands listed that will help marriage have a strong framework? (See page 58.)

Answer Key for Chapter 7 Discussion Questions

1. Unity is most vial, open communication and humbleness are very important as well (See page 53.)

2. Blame game (See page 54.)

3. Pay close attention to yourself and your teaching. (See page 54.)

4. Yes (See pages 54-55.)

5. Possess your authority with compassion and love and don't compromise the truth in the midst of opposition. (See page 55.)

6. Prayer (See page 56.)

7. To be in agreement with your husband concerning family matters, communicate love, provide support without criticism for your husband (See pages 56-57.)

8. By first changing ourselves with God's help (See page 57.)

9. All of you should be of one mind. Sympathize with each other. Love each other as brothers and sisters. Be tenderhearted, and keep a humble attitude. Don't repay evil for evil. Don't retaliate with insults when people insult you. Instead, pay them back with a blessing. (See page 58.)

Scripture References Chapter 7

1 TIMOTHY 4:16 NLT

Keep a close watch on how you live and on your teaching. Stay true to what is right for the sake of your own salvation and the salvation of those who hear you.

1 PETER 3:8-9 NLT

Finally, all of you should be of one mind. Sympathize with each other. Love each other as brothers and sisters. Be tenderhearted, and keep a humble attitude. Don't repay evil for evil. Don't retaliate with insults when people insult you. Instead, pay them back with a blessing. That is what God has called you to do, and he will grant you his blessing.

Chapter 8 Validating Without Celebrating

1. What is the most important to communicate to your children at any point of their lives? (See page 61.)
   a. That they need to make their bed
   b. That you ate too much pizza
   c. That you love them

2. What are people looking for in relationships? (See page 61.)
   a. Approval

b. Validation

c. Acceptance

d. Love

e. All of the above

3. What is validation? (See page 61.)

   a. Being good at math

   b. Being valued, feeling important, approved, confirmed

   c. It's a real estate term

4. It is important for parents to provide validation when a child is young. If validation is missing what do children typically do? (See page 61.)

   a. They ask you to have a talk with them

   b. They seek for approval and validation from other sources

   c. Nothing happens

5. What do the children struggling with sexuality want the most (deep inside)? (See page 62.)

   a. They want to feel loved and supported

   b. They want to brush and floss every night

   c. They want to study science

6. How can we validate our children without supporting their sinful lifestyle? (See page 63.)

   a. Compliment them on their accomplishments not related to their sinful lifestyle

   b. Praise their goals not related to their sinful lifestyle

   c. Validate who they are not related to their sinful lifestyle

   d. All of the above

7. Read Romans 2:4 in several translations. What helps people turn from sin? (See page 64.)

8. What is the best biblical response for the parent when the child shares that they are choosing homosexual lifestyle? (See page 64.)
    a.   Tell them that you are too busy to talk right now
    b.   Tell them you love them, that you will not disown them or reject them
    c.   Tell them what they are choosing is wrong in God's eyes
    d.   B and C

Answer Key for Chapter 8 Discussion Questions

1. c. That you love them (See page 61.)
2. e. All of the above (See page 61.)
3. b. Being valued, feeling important, approved, confirmed (See page 61.)
4. b. They seek approval and validation from other sources (See page 61.)
5. a. They want love and support (See page 62.)
6. d. All of the above. Validate who they are (their goals, talents, accomplishments), not because of their sinful choices or lifestyle. (See page 63.)
7. God's kindness, goodness, patience (See page 64.)
8. b and c. Use compassion without compromise and without discounting God's word. Assure the child that you love them and that you won't disown, reject or throw them out. See that God's truth and righteousness prevail. Communicate that you are not rejecting them. Don't make them feel alone or like strangers or outsiders. (See page 64.)

Scripture References Chapter 8

ROMANS 2:4 NLT

Don't you see how wonderfully kind, tolerant, and patient God is with you? Does this mean nothing to you? Can't you see that his kindness is intended to turn you from your sin?

ROMANS 2:4 AMPC

Or are you [so blind as to] trifle with and presume upon and despise and underestimate the wealth of His kindness and forbearance and long-suffering patience? Are you unmindful or actually ignorant [of the fact] that God's kindness is intended to lead you to repent (to change your mind and inner man to accept God's will)?

ROMANS 2:4 NIV

Or do you show contempt for the riches of his kindness, forbearance and patience, not realizing that God's kindness is intended to lead you to repentance?

ROMANS 2:4 NKJV

Or do you despise the riches of His goodness, forbearance, and longsuffering, not knowing that the goodness of God leads you to repentance?

Chapter 9 Establishing Boundaries

1. What is one of the most important things that parents need when establishing boundaries with children who are in a homosexual relationship? (See page 65.)

2. Read Galatians 1:10. Who are we to please as Christians?

3. What is number-one priority to follow when setting boundaries for children who are in a homosexual relationship? (See page 65.)

    a. Act and speak in a way pleasing to God

    b. Eat popcorn every day

    c. Allow the children to do whatever pleases them

4. What is a recommended boundary in chapter 9 when it comes to letting son's or daughter's partner to visit or spend the night? (See page 66.)

5. What would allowing the partner to visit or spend the night communicate to the child? (See page 66.)

6. How should the child's partner be treated? (See page 66.)

7. Is it important to keep the relationship with your loved one as strong as possible despite the disagreement? (See page 66.)

8. What is one way to strengthen the relationship? (See page 66.)

9. What is the recommended boundary in chapter 9 when it comes to having a grown child that does not live with you visit your home? (See page 67.)

10. What is the recommended boundary in chapter 9 for the grown child that doesn't live at home wanting to visit with the partner? (See page 67.)

11. What is the recommended boundary when it comes to deciding whether to attend the wedding of a homosexual child? (See pages 67-68.)

12. What kind of response to the invitation to the same-sex wedding is suggested in chapter 9? (See page 68.)

13. What is one of the most important things you can tell your children living in a homosexual lifestyle? (See page 68.).

14. Read Mark 4:17. Why does persecution comes? (See page 69.)

15. Read John 15:20. Is it normal for Christians to be persecuted because of their belief in Jesus and the Bible? (See page 69.)

16. Read Mark 4:17. What do some people do when persecution comes their way? (See page 69.)

17. How can you keep yourself strong as a Christian? (See pages 69-70.)

   a. Keep your relationship with God strong

b.   Read the Bible and pray every day

c.   Attend a Bible-believing church

d.   Attend a small group or a Bible study

e.   All of the above

18. What is the underlying principle that should guide you in making decisions related to child's lifestyle choice? (See page 70.)

a.   Compassion without compromise

b.   Rejection with anger

c.   The silent treatment

d.   None of the above

Answer Key for Chapter 9 Discussion Questions

1.   Wisdom given by the Holy Spirit and God's word (See page 65.)

2.   We are to please God.

3.   Act and speak in a way pleasing to God. (See page 65.)

4.   Not allow to visit or spend the night (See page 66.)

5.   It would communicate approval of the relationship even if that is not the intent. (See page 66.)

6.   With unconditional love (See page 66.)

7.   Yes (See page 66.)

8.   Spend quality time together. (See page 66.)

9.   All children should be allowed to come home. (See page 67.)

10. Not appropriate to allow the child to visit with the partner. Allowing it communicates the approval of the lifestyle whether it is intended or not. (See page 67.)

11. Participating in the civil union would be a violation of Scripture. Marriage is designed by God to be between a man and a woman. (See pages 67-68.)

12. Respectfully decline and you can go on to explain that you love them very much and that you cannot support a marriage that was not designed by God. (See page 68.)

13. That you love them and you are praying for them (See page 68.)

14. Because of the Word of God (See page 69.)

15. Yes, it's normal (See page 69.)

16. They fall away (See page 69.)

17. e. All of the above (See pages 69-70.)

18. a. Compassion without compromise (See page 70.)

Scripture References Chapter 9

GALATIANS 1:10 NIV

Am I now trying to win the approval of human beings, or of God? Or am I trying to please people? If I were still trying to please people, I would not be a servant of Christ.

MARK 4:17 NLT

But since they don't have deep roots, they don't last long. They fall away as soon as they have problems or are persecuted for believing God's word.

JOHN 15:20 NLT

Do you remember what I told you? "A slave is not greater than the master." Since they persecuted me, naturally they will persecute you. And if they had listened to me, they would listen to you.

Chapter 10 Parents Persevere

1. What is one of the greatest tools that the enemy uses to discourage people from believing? (See page 71.)
    a. Encouragement
    b. Discouragement
    c. Blessings
    d. None of the above

2. Read Joshua 1:9. What are we commanded to do? (See page 77.)

3. Read Joshua 1:9. Why are we commanded to be strong and courageous? (See page 71.)

4. Read Luke 18:1. What are we to do? (See page 71.)

5. What Old Testament heroes of faith are mentioned in this chapter? (See page 72.)
   a. Ruth and David
   b. Adam and Eve
   c. Abraham and Moses

6. Can you see yourself being like Abraham or Moses and believing without giving up?

7. Who can help us stand strong on a daily basis? (See page 72.)
   a. City mayor
   b. The postal service worker
   c. God and His Word

8. Read John 14:16. What is the Holy Spirit called? (See page 73.)

9. Read Exodus 34:6. What does it say about the Lord? Has God been patient with you?

10. Read the list of "We will not give up..." statements on page 74. Which one encourages you the most?

11. What are the 3 things we are to do when we make a determination to follow the path God has called us to? (See page 74.)
    a. Never stop eating pizza, drinking pop and eating cookies
    b. Never stop making the bed, washing dishes and folding laundry
    c. Never stop praying, never stop believing, never stop seeking God

12. What are the parents in ministry encouraged to do if they have children who have chosen the homosexual lifestyle? (See pages 75-76.)

   a. Continue to pursue the ministry God has called them to

   b. Quickly pack and move to another state

   c. Give up on the ministry God has called them to

Answer Key for Chapter 10 Discussion Questions

1. b. Discouragement (See page 71.)
2. To be strong and courageous (See page 71.)
3. For the Lord your God is with you. (See page 71.)
4. To pray and never lose heart or give up. (See page 71.)
5. c. Abraham and Moses (See page 72.)
6. Discussion question
7. c. God and His word (See page 73.)
8. Our Comforter (See page 73.)
9. He is patient.
10. Answers will vary (See page 74.)
11. c. Never stop praying, never stop believing, never stop seeking God. (See page 74.)
12. a. They are encouraged to continue to pursue the ministry God has called them to do. (See pages 75-76.)

Scripture References Chapter 10

JOSHUA 1:9 NLT

This is my command—be strong and courageous! Do not be afraid or discouraged. For the LORD your God is with you wherever you go.

LUKE 18:1 NIV

Then Jesus told his disciples a parable to show them that they should always pray and not give up.

JOHN 14:16 KJV

And I will pray the Father, and he shall give you another Comforter, that he may abide with you for ever.

EXODUS 34:6 NIV

And he passed in front of Moses, proclaiming, "The LORD, the LORD, the compassionate and gracious God, slow to anger, abounding in love and faithfulness."

Chapter 11 Working Through Grief

1. If a child tells the parent they are gay, what kind of response should the parents show? (See page 78.)
   a. Affirm the courage it took to share
   b. Do not show acceptance of the lifestyle
   c. Be empathetic and understanding
   d. Don't condone sin

2. Read Hebrews 4:15. Does Jesus understand our weaknesses? (See page 78.)

3. What are some of the actual words that you can say if someone tells you they are gay? Make sure they are full of love, compassion, and understanding without compromise.

4. What is paramount to keep open in your relationship with your children? (See page 78.)
   a. Keep all doors opened and unlocked
   b. Keep communication open
   c. Keep essential oil jars open

5. What should parents avoid as part of response? (See page 79.)

6. What might be needed of parents to ask their child? (See page 81.)
   a. Ask for a gift
   b. Ask for a pet

    c.   Ask for forgiveness

7. Read Ephesians 6:10. According to this verse what is important to do? (See page 82.)

8. What is one area to keep in mind pertaining to your child announcing to you they are gay when it comes to your marriage? (See page 82.)

9. Blame, finger-pointing and division in marriage can all hinder what? (See page 82.)

    a.   Divorce

    b.   Favorite sports team from winning

    c.   Real progress and healing

10. What is important to focus on instead in marriage? (See page 83.)

    a.   Spiritual wellbeing, unity, praying together as a family

    b.   Yelling and blaming each member of the family

    c.   Do nothing, just go on with life and stop talking to each other completely

11. Is it important and helpful to seek encouragement from godly people and your church? (See page 83.)

12. What was the most helpful for you to read about in this chapter?

Answer Key for Chapter 11 Discussion Questions

1. All answers apply (See page 78.)

2. Yes (See page 78.)

3. Answers will vary

4. b. Communication (See page 78.)

5. Anger (See page 79.)

6. c. Ask for forgiveness (See page 81.)

7. Stay strong in the Lord (See page 82.)

8. Avoid finger-pointing, division and blame (See page 82.)

9. c. Real progress and healing (See page 82.)

10. a. Spiritual wellbeing, unity, praying together as a family (See page 83.)

11. Yes (see page 83.)

12. Answers will vary

Scripture References Chapter 11

HEBREWS 4:15 NIV

For we do not have a high priest who is unable to empathize with our weaknesses, but we have one who has been tempted in every way, just as we are—yet he did not sin.

EPHESIANS 6:10 NIV

Finally, be strong in the Lord and in his mighty power.

Chapter 12 Praying Effectively

1. Is it important to acknowledge sin and accept responsibility for it? (See page 85.)

2. What should every Christian parent do regarding sexual sin in their family? (See page 85.)
   a. Ignore sin in your family
   b. Seek God's counsel, asking to reveal where to seek forgiveness from God, your child or yourself
   c. Write a blog about sin in the family

3. What does repentance help with? (See page 85.)
   a. Repentance is useless
   b. Repentance is a waste of time
   c. Repentance can help establish a foundation of love and forgiveness in a relationship

4. According to chapter 12, what should we always do first as an action to take after we have repented? (See page 85.)
   a. Get a box of cookies and eat them

b. Find someone to yell at

c. Pray to God

5. See pages 86 and 88. How should we pray to God?

a. Pray in faith, trusting and believing, pray daily.

b. Pray once a week when at church, that's good enough.

c. My child has made a decision, prayer won't help.

6. Review different suggestions and scriptures mentioned on prayer. Which one is the most meaningful to you?

Answer Key for Chapter 12 Discussion Questions

1. Yes (See page 85.)

2. b. Seek God's counsel, asking to reveal where to seek forgiveness from God, your child or yourself. (See page 85.)

3. c. Repentance can help establish a foundation of love and forgiveness in a relationship (See page 85.)

4. c. Pray to God. (See page 85.)

5. a. Pray in faith, trusting and believing, pray daily.

6. Answers will vary

Chapter 15 Sexual Sin Is Sin, Right?

1. In what context is a sexual relationship to be enjoyed according to the Bible? (See page 107.)

a. There are no guidelines about it in the Bible.

b. Within the context of man and woman in a marriage relationship

c. God leaves it up to you what you do with your body.

2. Why is it important to follow God's ways when it comes to sex? (See page 107.)

a. It's better for us.

b. It protects us from unwanted and painful consequences.

c. It is for our blessing in this area

3. In our current culture, is there a clear definition of what sexual sin is? (See page 107.)
    a. No
    b. Yes
    c. Not sure

4. Read James 1:14-15. Where does temptation start? (See page 108.)

5. What should we desire instead of temptation and sin? (See page 108.)
    a. Eat more and sleep more
    b. Watch more TV
    c. Seek after God

6. Are there other sexual sins mentioned in the Bible that should also be preached against? (See page 109.)

7. Read 1 Corinthians 6:18, Deuteronomy 22:22, Exodus 22:19, Deuteronomy 5:18, Deuteronomy 22:25-29, Leviticus 18:6-18. What sexual sins are described here? (See page 109.)
    a. Fornication
    b. Premarital sex
    c. Bestiality
    d. Adultery
    e. Rape
    f. Incest

8. What does God call us to instead of sin? (See page 109.)
    a. Freedom of choice
    b. Purity and righteousness
    c. Sin as much as we want

9. What should we do as Christians according to chapter 15 on page 109?
    a. Stand up for what is right

b. Lay low and do nothing

c. Mind your own business

10. How can Christian parents stand up for what is right? (See page 109.)

a. Live a godly life

b. Know God

c. Know what God's word says

11. How can Christian parents help children see what is sin? (See page 109.)

a. By telling them to watch more TV

b. By teaching them what the Bible says

c. Let the society teach them about sin

12. How can a Christian parent help their child see that their sexual behavior is sin? (See page 109.)

a. Hold them accountable

b. Don't allow sin into your home

c. Don't condone their behavior

13. What are the most important attitudes to have as a Christian toward other people? (See pages 109-110.)

a. Harshness

b. Love and compassion

c. Sadness

Answer Key for Chapter 15 Discussion Questions

1. b. Within the context of man and woman in a marriage relationship (See page 107.)

2. All answers are correct (See page 107.)

3. a. no (See page 107.)

4. Temptation starts in our desires (See page 108.)

5. c. Seek after God (See page 108.)

6. Yes (See page 109.)

7. All answers apply (See page 109.)

8. b. Purity and righteousness (See page 109.)

9. a. Stand up for what is right (See page 109.)

10. All answers are correct (See page 109.)

11. b. By teaching them what the Bible says (See page 109.)

12. All answers are correct (See page 109.)

13. b. Love and compassion (See pages 109-110.)

Scripture References Chapter 15

JAMES 1:14-15 NLT

Temptation comes from our own desires, which entice us and drag us away. These desires give birth to sinful actions. And when sin is allowed to grow, it gives birth to death.

1 CORINTHIANS 6:18 KJV

Flee fornication. Every sin that a man doeth is without the body; but he that committeth fornication sinneth against his own body.

DEUTERONOMY 22:13-21 NLT

Suppose a man marries a woman, but after sleeping with her, he turns against her and publicly accuses her of shameful conduct, saying, "When I married this woman, I discovered she was not a virgin." Then the woman's father and mother must bring the proof of her virginity to the elders as they hold court at the town gate. Her father must say to them, "I gave my daughter to this man to be his wife, and now he has turned against her. He has accused her of shameful conduct, saying, 'I discovered that your daughter was not a virgin.' But here is the proof of my daughter's virginity." Then they must spread her bed sheet before the elders. The elders must then take the man and punish him. They must also fine him 100 pieces of silver, which he must pay to the woman's father because he publicly accused a virgin of Israel of shameful conduct. The woman will then remain the man's wife, and he may never divorce her. But suppose the man's accusations are true, and he can show that she was not a virgin. The woman must be taken to the door of her father's home, and there the men of the town must stone her to death, for she has committed a disgraceful crime in Israel by being promiscuous while living in her parents' home. In this way, you will purge this evil from among you.

EXODUS 22:19 NLT

Anyone who has sexual relations with an animal must certainly be put to death.

DEUTERONOMY 5:18 NLT

You must not commit adultery.

DEUTERONOMY 22:25-29 NLT

But if the man meets the engaged woman out in the country, and he rapes her, then only the man must die. Do nothing to the young woman; she has committed no crime worthy of death. She is as innocent as a murder victim. Since the man raped her out in the country, it must be assumed that she screamed, but there was no one to rescue her. Suppose a man has intercourse with a young woman who is a virgin but is not engaged to be married. If they are discovered, he must pay her father fifty pieces of silver. Then he must marry the young woman because he violated her, and he may never divorce her as long as he lives.

LEVITICUS 18:6-18 NLT

You must never have sexual relations with a close relative, for I am the Lord. Do not violate your father by having sexual relations with your mother. She is your mother; you must not have sexual relations with her. Do not have sexual relations with any of your father's wives, for this would violate your father. Do not have sexual relations with your sister or half sister, whether she is your father's daughter or your mother's daughter, whether she was born into your household or someone else's. Do not have sexual relations with your granddaughter, whether she is your son's daughter or your daughter's daughter, for this would violate your-self. Do not have sexual relations with your stepsister, the daughter of any of your father's wives, for she is your sister. Do not have sexual relations with your father's sister, for she is your father's close relative. Do not have sexual relations with your mother's sister, for she is your mother's close relative. Do not violate your uncle, your father's brother, by having sexual relations with his wife, for she is your aunt. Do not have sexual relations with your daughter-in-law; she is your son's wife, so you must not have sexual relations with her. Do not have sexual relations with your brother's wife, for this would violate your brother. Do not have sexual relations with both a woman and her daughter. And do not take her granddaughter, whether her son's daughter or her daughter's daugh-ter, and have sexual relations with her. They are close relatives, and this would be a wicked act. While your wife is living, do not marry her sister and have sexual relations with her, for they would be rivals.

Chapter 16 The Judgmental Church

1. According to chapter 16, what is the Church's responsibility on the earth? (See page 111.)
   a. To be an entertainment venue
   b. To be a reflection of God to everyone who observes it
   c. To be a hangout place for old people

2. As individual Christians who do we reveal to the people we come in contact with? (See page 111.)
   a. We reveal Christ
   b. We reveal nothing
   c. We reveal the wrath

3. True or False: The Church and individual Christians have not lived up to the responsibility of representing Christ in response to homosexuality. (See page 111.)

4. Read 2 Corinthians 5:20. What are Christians called? (See page 111.)

5. Read 1 Timothy 3:15. What is the Church of the living God called? (See page 111.)

6. Read Revelation 2:4. What did the church left? (See page 111.)

7. Jesus is calling us to what? (See page 112.)

    a. To find a new way to heaven

    b. To effectively blend in

    c. Return to our first love and do the deeds we did when we first became believers

8. What are two wrong approaches the Church has taken toward homosexuals? (See page 112.)

    a. Judgment and condemnation

    b. Accepted and welcomed homosexuals to pulpits

    c. Both A and B

9. What should be the motivation for teaching about sin according to chapter 16? (See page 113.)

    a. Fear and dread

    b. Love and grace

    c. Fun and games

10. Read 1 Samuel 16:7. What is more important to God, the outer appearance, or the heart? (See page 113.)

11. Read Luke 19:10. What is Jesus' purpose on the earth? (See page 114.)

12. Read Romans 5:8. What were we when God showed His great love for us? (See page 114.)

13. What kind of attitude should Christians have toward unlovely? (See page 114.)

    a. Judgment and condemnation

    b. Wonder and amazement

    c. Love and compassion

14. Read John 13:35. How can people tell that we are disciples of Jesus? (See pages 117-118.)

15. What two banners mentioned in chapter 16 is the Church supposed to hold up? (See page 119.)
    a. Banners of entertainment and TV
    b. Banners of fishing and hunting
    c. Banner of truth and love

Answer Key for Chapter 16 Discussion Questions

1. b. To be a reflection of God to everyone who observes it (See page 111.)

2. a. We reveal Christ (See page 111.)

3. True (See page 111.)

4. Christ's ambassadors (See page 111.)

5. The pillar and the foundation of the truth (See page 111.)

6. Left first love (See page 111.)

7. c. To return to our first love and do the deeds we did when we first became believers (See page 112.)

8. c. Both a and b (See page 112.)

9. b. Love and grace (See page 113.)

10. The heart (See page 113.)

11. Seek and save the lost (See page 114.)

12. We were still sinners (See page 114.)

13. c. Love and compassion (See page 116.)

14. Our love for one another (See pages 117-118.)

15. c. Banners of truth and love (See page 119.)

Scripture References Chapter 16

2 CORINTHIANS 5:20 NIV

We are therefore Christ's ambassadors, as though God were making his appeal through us. We implore you on Christ's behalf: Be reconciled to God.

1 TIMOTHY 3:15 NLT

So that if I am delayed, you will know how people must conduct themselves in the household of God. This is the church of the living God, which is the pillar and foundation of the truth.

REVELATION 2:4 NKJV

Nevertheless I have this against you, that you have left your first love.

1 SAMUEL 16:7 NIV

But the LORD said to Samuel, "Do not consider his appearance or his height, for I have rejected him. The LORD does not look at the things people look at. People look at the outward appearance, but the LORD looks at the heart."

LUKE 19:10 NIV

For the Son of Man came to seek and to save the lost.

ROMANS 5:8 NLT

But God showed his great love for us by sending Christ to die for us while we were still sinners.

JOHN 13:35 NLT

Your love for one another will prove to the world that you are my disciples.

Chapter 17 How to Minister as the Church

1. Read Mark 16:15 and Matthew 28:19. What did Jesus instruct His disciples and us to do? (See page 121.)

2. What should we exemplify when ministering to homosexuals? (See page 122.)

a. Love and compassion

b. Fruit and nuts

c. Don't minister to the homosexuals

3. What are three points to remember when helping someone change according to Chapter 17? (See pages 122-123.)

4. What is the ultimate goal when helping the homosexual? (See page 124.)

5. What is a major key to teach an individual who is leaving a sinful lifestyle? (See page 125.)

a. Chew more gum

b. Teach them to fly an airplane

c. Teach them who they are in Christ

6. For the person struggling, it is important to see himself/herself in what way? (See page 125.)

7. Read the story of the missionary to the gay community. What are your thoughts on that? (See pages 126-128.)

Answer Key for Chapter 17 Discussion Questions

1. Preach the gospel to all creation and make disciples (See page 121.)

2. a. Love and compassion (See page 122.)

3. Choice must be theirs alone, process requires leaving the old behind, surround the person with support (See pages 123-124.)

4. To see the person walk into wholeness and obedience (See page 125.)

5. c. Teach them who they are in Christ (See page 125.)

6. To see himself the way God sees him (See page 125.)

7. Answers will vary (See pages 126-128.)

Scripture References Chapter 17

MARK 16:15 NIV

He said to them, "Go into all the world and preach the gospel to all creation."

MATTHEW 28:19 NLT

Therefore, go and make disciples of all the nations, baptizing them in the name of the Father and the Son and the Holy Spirit.

Chapter 18 Prayer

1. Read 2 Corinthians 4:4. Who is the god of this world?

2. According to 2 Corinthians 4:4, what is the god of this world doing to nonbelievers? (See page 130.)

3. What is Satan trying to do by blinding the minds of those who don't believe? (See page 130.)

4. Read 1 Corinthians 2:14. What is one of the reasons that people can't receive truths from God's Spirit? (See page 131.)

5. Read Matthew 9:35-38. What did Jesus command to do?

6. Who are the harvest in Matthew 9:35-38?

7. How are we to pray for the lost? (See page 131.)

8. Read Luke 15:4 and Revelation 3:20 about God's heart for the lost. How can you describe God's heart for the lost according to these passages? (See page 134.)

9. Read James 5:16. What does it say about prayer? (See page 134.)

10. What does the Greek word *fervent* mean? (See page 134.)

11. Read Philippians 4:6, Colossians 4:2 and 1 Timothy 2:1. What are we commanded to do?

12. Read Luke 18:1. What are we commanded to do?

13. Read Galatians 6:9. If we don't give up what will happen?

14. Read John 15:7. What is the promise that Jesus promises in this verse? (See page 136.)

Answer Key for Chapter 18 Discussion Questions

1. Satan.

2. Is blinding their minds. (See page 130.)

3. Satan is keeping them from seeing the glorious light of the Good News. (See page 130.)

4. It all sounds foolish to them and they can't understand it. (See page 131.)

5. Pray for the Lord of the harvest to send workers into the fields.

6. People who need Jesus are the harvest.

7. We are to pray according to God's word. (See page 131.)

8. God will search for the one lost sheep and He will keep pursuing or knocking to be with them. (See page 134.)

9. The effective, fervent prayer of a righteous man avails much. (See page 138.)

10. The Greek word for *fervent* means to be active and efficient. (See page 134.)

11. To pray.

12. To pray and not lose heart.

13. We will reap a harvest.

14. Ask what you desire and it shall be done for you. (See page 136.)

Scripture References Chapter 18

2 CORINTHIANS 4:4 NLT

Satan, who is the god of this world, has blinded the minds of those who don't believe. They are unable to see the glorious light of the Good News. They don't understand this message about the glory of Christ, who is the exact likeness of God.

1 CORINTHIANS 2:14 NLT

But people who aren't spiritual can't receive these truths from God's Spirit. It all sounds foolish to them and they can't understand it, for only those who are spiritual can understand what the Spirit means.

MATTHEW 9:38 NLT

Jesus traveled through all the towns and villages of that area, teaching in the synagogues and announcing the Good News about the Kingdom. And he healed every kind of disease and illness. When he saw the crowds, he had compassion on them because they were confused and helpless, like sheep without a shepherd. He said to his disciples, "The harvest is great, but the workers are few. So pray to the Lord who is in charge of the harvest; ask him to send more workers into his fields."

LUKE 15:4 NLT

If a man has a hundred sheep and one of them gets lost, what will he do? Won't he leave the ninety-nine others in the wilderness and go to search for the one that is lost until he finds it?

REVELATION 3:20 NLT

Look! I stand at the door and knock. If you hear my voice and open the door, I will come in, and we will share a meal together as friends.

JAMES 5:16 NKJV

Confess your trespasses to one another, and pray for one another, that you may be healed. The effective, fervent prayer of a righteous man avails much.

PHILIPPIANS 4:6 NIV

Do not be anxious about anything, but in every situation, by prayer and petition, with thanksgiving, present your requests to God.

COLOSSIANS 4:2 NIV

Devote yourselves to prayer, being watchful and thankful.

1 TIMOTHY 2:1 NIV

I urge, then, first of all, that petitions, prayers, intercession and thanksgiving be made for all people.

LUKE 18:1 NKJV

Then He spoke a parable to them, that men always ought to pray and not lose heart.

GALATIANS 6:9 NIV

Let us not become weary in doing good, for at the proper time we will reap a harvest if we do not give up.

JOHN 15:7 NKJV

If you abide in Me, and My words abide in you, you will ask what you desire, and it shall be done for you.

Chapter 19 Dear Pastor

1. Homosexuality is what type of a crisis? (See page 138.)
   a. Cupcake crisis
   b. Sexuality crisis
   c. Identity crisis

2. The church ought to be a place of gathering where struggling people can be set free from what? (See page 138.).:
   a. Homophobia
   b. Homosexuality
   c. Transgenderism
   d. All of the above

3. Read Hebrews 4:12. What exposes the innermost thoughts and desires? (See page 139.)

4. According to chapter 19, what kind of guidance from the Church would really help people struggling with homosexuality? (See page 139.)

5. According to chapter 19, who do the pastors, ministry leaders, deacons and the leaders in the church minister to? (See page 140.)
   a. Only people that are taller than 6 feet
   b. Only people that chew gum
   c. All

6. How should the Church minister to the people? (See page 140.)
   a. With gentleness and grace
   b. With guilt and condemnation
   c. With anger and wrath

7. According to chapter 19, what is important to remember when ministering to those struggling with homosexuality? (See page 141.)
   a. Eating turkey on Thanksgiving is a choice
   b. Driving backwards is a temptation
   c. Sexual identity is a choice, same-sex attraction is a temptation

8. According to chapter 19, what should be the focus when ministering to the person struggling with homosexuality? (See page 141.)

9. What is the pastor equipped to do for the body of Christ? (See page 142.)
   a. To host weekly movie nights
   b. To empower the body of Christ
   c. To vacuum the church

10. What is the pastor encouraged to heavily rely on when ministering? (See page 142.)
    a. His gym membership
    b. His Sam's Club membership
    c. The resurrection power of God

11. Of the Holy Trinity who does the transforming work in every person? (See page 146.)

Answer Key for Chapter 19 Discussion Questions

1. c. Identity crisis (See page 138.)
2. d. All of the above (See page 138.)
3. The word of God (See page 139.)
4. Spiritual and sexual guidance (See page 139.)
5. c. All (See page 140.)
6. a. With gentleness and grace (See page 140.)
7. c. Sexual identity is a choice, same-sex attraction is a temptation (See page 141.)
8. The focus should be on their spirituality (See page 141.)
9. b. To empower the body of Christ (See page 141.)
10. c. The resurrection power of God (See page 142.)
11. The Holy Spirit. (See page 142.)

Scripture References Chapter 19

HEBREWS 4:12 NLT

For the word of God is alive and powerful. It is sharper than the sharpest two-edged sword, cutting between soul and spirit, between joint and marrow. It exposes our innermost thoughts and desires.

About the Author

Janet Boynes founded Janet Boynes Ministries in Maple Grove, Minnestoa, in 2006. She authored the books: *Called Out—A Former Lesbian's Discovery of Freedom, Arise—The Journey from Fear to Faith,* and *God & Sexuality—Truth & Relevance Without Compromise.* She challenges individuals and the church to reach out with a message of hope and restoration to those who struggle with identity issues.

Her articles have appeared in *Charisma Magazine, Believer's Voice of Victory Magazine* and many more. Her life is proof that the love of God has the power to heal and restore the brokenness in our lives. It's been over twenty years since she was called out of the lesbian lifestyle. Janet is an ordained minister under the Assemblies of God and travels the United States and overseas sharing a message of redemption. Her desire is to bring hope through the power of Jesus Christ.

OUR VISION

Proclaiming the truth and the power of the Gospel of Jesus Christ with excellence. Challenging Christians to live victoriously, grow spiritually, know God intimately.

Connect with us on

Facebook @ **HarrisonHousePublishers**

and Instagram @ **HarrisonHousePublishing**

so you can stay up to date with news about our books and our authors.

Visit us at **www.harrisonhouse.com** for a complete product listing as well as monthly specials for wholesale distribution.